CUR
26843
LOF
2002

W9-ABR-881

LIVING Our FAITH
Morality
Challenges and Choices

Principal **Consultants**

Dennis J. Bozanich, MBA

Michael Carotta, EdD

Rev. Leonard Wenke, MDiv

Lourdes Library
Gwynedd Mercy College
DISCARD
P. O. Box 901
Gwynedd Valley, PA 19437-0901

Principal **Reviewers**

Mary Lee Becker, MPM

Robert J. Kealey, EdD

M. Annette Mandley-Turner, MS

DISCARD
LOURDES LIBRARY
CURRICULUM COLLECTION

Harcourt
Religion Publishers

Nihil Obstat
Rev. Richard L. Schaefer
Censor Deputatus

Imprimatur
✠ Most Rev. Jerome Hanus, OSB
Archbishop of Dubuque
January 31, 2001
Feast of Saint John Bosco, Patron of Youth and Catholic Publishers

The nihil obstat and imprimatur are official declarations that a book or pamphlet is free of doctrinal or moral error. No implication is contained herein that those who granted the nihil obstat and imprimatur agree with the contents, opinions, or statements expressed.

Our Mission
The primary mission of Harcourt Religion Publishers is to provide the Catholic and Christian educational markets with the highest quality catechetical print and media resources. The content of these resources reflects the best insights of current theology, methodology, and pedagogical research. These resources are practical and easy to use, designed to meet expressed market needs, and written to reflect the teachings of the Catholic Church.

Copyright © 2002 by Harcourt Religion Publishers, a division of Harcourt, Inc.

All rights reserved. No part of this publication may be reproduced or transmitted in any form or by any means, electronic or mechanical, including photocopy, recording, or any information storage and retrieval system, without permission in writing from the publisher.

Requests for permission to make copies of any part of this work should be mailed to Permissions Department, Harcourt, Inc., 6277 Sea Harbor Drive, Orlando, Florida 32887-6777.

New Revised Standard Version Bible: Catholic Edition copyright © 1993 and 1989 by the Division of Christian Education of the National Council of the Churches of Christ in the U.S.A. Used by permission. All rights reserved.

Photography Credits
AP Wide World Photos: Alan Mothner: 59; Angelo Scipioni: 77; **Art Resource:** Erich Lessing: 99; **Catholic News Service:** 39; The Crosiers: 37; Nancy Wiechec: 38; **Bridgeman Art Library:** Musee National d'ArtModerne, Paris, France/Peter Willi/©2000 Artist Rights Society, New York/ADAGP, Paris: 84; **The Crosiers:** Gene Plaisted: 8, 17, 29, 39, 55, 63, 94; **Digital Imaging Group:** Erik Snowbeck: 37; **Digital Vision Ltd.:** 16, 18, 75, 100; **FPG International:** 8; Jim Cummins: 65; Kevin Laubacher: 80; Dick Luria: 5; Stephen Simpson: 14; Arthur Tilley: 44, 90; Telegraph Colour Library: 4, 65, 85; VCG: 67, 69; **Jack Holtel:** 15, 47, 54, 57, 58, 70, 71, 77; **Image Bank:** Color Day: 33; L. D. Gordon: 59; Jack Kurtz: 9; Guido A. Rossi: 18; Nicolas Russell: 5; **Impact Visuals:** Jack Kurtz: 9; *juliana@tin.it, http://www.umilta.net:* 47; **Masterfile:** Larry Williams: 36; **Nicholas Studios:** Nick Falzerano: 6, 16, 45; **PhotoDisc, Inc.:** 34, 46, 64, 70, 76, 80; **Photo Edit:** Jose Carrillo: 19; Myrleen Ferguson Cate: 58, 64, 65, 99; Richard Hutchings: 97; Michael Newman: 64, 89, 98, 99; Jonathan Nourok: 37; Alan Oddie: 57, 79; David Young-Wolff: 67, 68; **Photo Researchers:** Earl Roberge: 15; **Picture Quest:** David Young-Wolff/PhotoEdit: 22; **Rock Stream Studios:** 27; **Skjold Photographs:** 49, 65, 96, 101; **Stock Boston:** Bob Daemmrich: 41; **The Stock Market:** ChromoSohm: 85; Charles Gupton: 72; Ted Horowitz: 65; Bob Krist: 78; Gabe Palmer: 12, 85; J. Polleross: 88; Sanford/Agliolo: 102; George Shelley: 5; Tom Stewart: 11, 66; **Stone:** Bruce Ayres: 89; Hulton Getty: 9; Paul Harris: 61; Walter Hodges: 34; Ed Honowitz: 74; Billy Hustace: 51; Andy Sacks: 48; David Young-Wolff: 5, 94; **SuperStock:** 83, 85; **Westminster Abbey Library:** Dean and Chapter of Westminster, London: 89; **Jim Whitmer Photography:** Jim Whitmer: 5, 24, 56; **W. P. Wittman Photography:** Bill Wittman: 97; **Wonderfile:** 20, 30, 44, 71, 92

Cover Photos
The Crosiers: Gene Plaisted; **Jack Holtel**

Feature Icons
Catholics Believe: Jack Holtel; **Opening the Word:** PictureQuest; **Our Christian Journey:** PictureQuest: Chuck Fishman/Contact Press Images

Location and Props
Dayton Church Supply; St. Christopher Catholic School, Vandalia, OH; St. Peter Catholic School, Huber Heights, OH

Printed in the United States of America

ISBN 0-15-900512-4

10   9   8   7   6

LIVING Our FAITH
Morality
Challenges and Choices

CHAPTER 1

In God's Image

Most holy God, you created us in your own image. Help us use the gifts you have given us to grow closer to you and to show others the power of your love. In Jesus' name we pray. Amen.

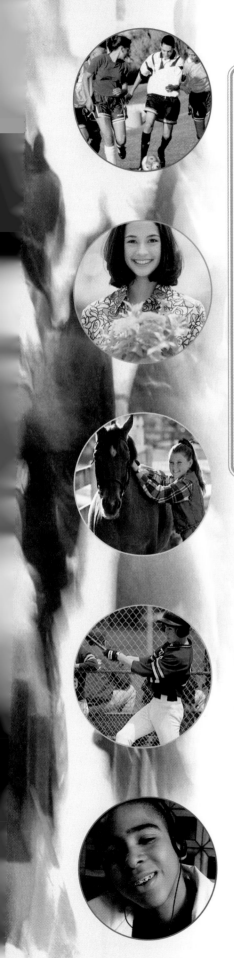

Answer the questions below.

God created only one you. What makes you unique?

What do you think God wants from you?

1) _____

_____

_____

2) _____

_____

_____

Created as
Unique

Think of people you know: family, friends, classmates. There may be some similarities among these people, but no two are exactly alike. Each is a one-of-a-kind combination of gifts and abilities.

Perhaps even more amazing is the fact that we are not alone in our uniqueness. Individuality is found in all species of animals and plants, down to the smallest blade of grass.

And yet despite this diversity, there is order to the universe. There are certain patterns, like the seasons, that occur without fail. There are certain physical laws, like gravity, that always apply.

Equal in Love

Humanity's special place in creation is marked by these qualities: We are created in the image of God. We are body and spirit. We have been created for friendship with God.

The creation stories found in the Book of Genesis state that God created man and woman in his image. (See *Genesis 1:27*.) Being made in the image of God gives each person **dignity.** We are worthy of respect because we are not just some*thing,* but some*one.* We must respect others and ourselves because all of us are sons or daughters of God.

in God's image

worthy of respect

dignity

Opening the Word

1st Sunday of Lent, Cycle C

For there is no distinction between Jew and Greek; the same Lord is Lord of all and is generous to all who call on him. For, "Everyone who calls on the name of the Lord shall be saved." Romans 10:12–13

Read *Romans 10* as well as *Genesis 1:27, Joel 2:32,* and *1 Corinthians 12:12–13.* How can I live the message of unity illustrated in these passages?

_____
_____
_____
_____

Body and Spirit

Our unity of body and spirit makes us truly human. All creatures, from beetles to blue whales, have bodies. But only humans are created with immortal souls. Indeed, it is the spirit, the deepest part of ourselves, that is most truly in the image of God and that most clearly defines who we really are. Our gifts, talents, and personality traits that make us unique are the expressions of our spirits. Think about it. It is not hair color, complexion, or height that defines who we are in the eyes of God. It is our spirit. In fact, the Church teaches that our souls were created by God when we were conceived.

Each One of Us

Each of us is a child of God and in God's eyes all of us have **equality** and dignity. Every person, regardless of gender, race, or background, deserves respect. As people of faith we are called to respect and treat others with dignity.

There are many ways that we are different. There are many types of physical differences in humans. We differ also in our personalities and abilities. It is this diversity of abilities and personalities that helps us work together. We need one another physically and mentally, emotionally, and spiritually.

Sometimes it might seem easy or even desirable to stereotype people into groups. If we did, we could easily determine what a person was like and how we could relate to him or her. But if we did that, we would fail to know the true person. For example, sometimes people with glasses are stereotyped as being intelligent. If you held to that presumption and met someone with glasses, you might feel as though you weren't smart enough to try to be that person's friend. You could be missing out on a good friendship. It is that true person with unique abilities and personality traits that we need to discover.

Focus On

Stereotypes

Stereotyping happens in many different ways. We most often think of racial slurs or degrading gender comments as being the only forms of stereotyping. However, we need to remember that making generalizations about groups of people, whether meant to be cruel or not, is a type of prejudice. All women do not cook well, and all men are not strong and athletic.

Share with your Faith Partner examples of "innocent" stereotyping. How might this type of stereotyping be harmful?

FaiTH PaRTNeRSHiP

Created for Covenant

God desires to communicate his own life to humans. There have been many times when God could have abandoned humanity. Instead, God offered salvation and established a *covenant,* or sacred promise, with humanity. This promise reminds us that God is in a relationship with us. And the fact that God's salvation came through his Son Jesus reveals just how far God will go to be with us. Imagine how much God must love us to become one of us and to live and die among us!

God calls us to deepen our relationship with him. God wants so much for us to remain with him that he gives **grace,** or his life in us through the Holy Spirit. This grace is a freely given gift from God, available to all. There is nothing we can do to earn or deserve grace, but we need grace if we are to respond to God's call in our lives. Once we have opened our hearts to God, the power of the Holy Spirit moves us to seek the grace needed for eternal life. Through prayer and the sacraments, we deepen our relationship with God. The same grace that allows us to respond to God also leads us to **faith.** This gift from God is the desire to seek out God and believe in him.

The more we believe in God, the more we seek to understand him; and the more we understand him, the more we seek to believe and the more we are set afire by love. See Catechism, #158.

What things in your life help strengthen your faith?

_____

_____

_____

When we are aware of God in our lives, we can sense the beauty that is all around us. Think of a time when you felt very happy. The sun probably seemed to shine brighter or the grass seemed greener. The same slanted perspective can happen when you are sad or depressed. Even the most perfect day seems dreary when you are miserable. If we accept God's grace and faith, we allow ourselves to be filled with his love. And filled with his love, even an awful situation won't be too awful, because along with love comes hope, comfort, and the faith that God is present with you.

To be fully alive, we need to recognize our place as a son or daughter of God and to accept the grace and faith that allow us to grow closer to him. Grace and faith lead us to use our gifts and abilities for the good of others. If you play a musical instrument, perhaps you can play for someone who needs some enjoyment. Or maybe you can organize your group of friends to do yardwork for older people in your neighborhood. Remember, the best way for us to glorify God is to use the gifts he has given us by living up to our full potential. We begin to truly live only when we give back to God what he has first given to us.

Living the life God wants for us can be very demanding. Loving our enemies, turning the other cheek, and picking up our own crosses may even sound impossible. It is not easy to sit in class next to someone with whom you have had an argument. You might be distracted or you might even want to say something mean. But by returning and by not giving in to revengeful behavior, you will learn how to get past angry feelings and you may even be able to rekindle your friendship.

There are many challenges and choices we face along the way to God. And there are also many paths that lead away from God. Many of these paths, such as underage drinking and partying with friends, seem inviting. But participating in activities like this can lead to drinking problems or other situations in which you don't have total control of your actions. If a path is not leading us closer to God, it is leading us to problems and a life without love. Fortunately, we are not in this life alone. Besides creating us for himself, God created us as part of a community. God places us in the midst of others so we can love and support each other on our journeys toward God and the fullness of his kingdom.

OUR CHRISTIAN JOURNEY

Understanding Faith

Clive Staples (C. S.) Lewis was a great defender of the Christian faith. Born in 1898 in Britain, C. S. Lewis was an atheist, someone who denies the existence of God, for much of his young life. When he converted to Christianity as an adult, he became a powerful voice for God. Lewis devoted much of his adult life to writing and speaking about matters of faith, putting very complicated ideas into words that people of all ages could understand.

In one of his most famous works, *Mere Christianity,* Lewis wrote about faith being a gift from God. According to Lewis, once we discover that we cannot earn grace and that even faith comes from God, then we become open to God working in our lives. After this "awakening" we can truly live.

For further information: Read some of Lewis's works of fiction, such as his Space Trilogy: *Out of the Silent Planet, Perelandra,* and *That Hideous Strength.* Lewis uses many aspects of religious truth as analogies even in his fiction.

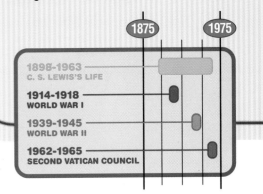

1875   1975

1898-1963
C. S. LEWIS'S LIFE

1914-1918
WORLD WAR I

1939-1945
WORLD WAR II

1962-1965
SECOND VATICAN COUNCIL

In Community

God himself is a communion—Father, Son, and Spirit. He is three Persons so closely united that they are indeed one God.

The communities to which we belong need to reflect the communion of the Holy Trinity. We are created for community, and we are drawn to seek this unity with others.

The most important community to which we belong is our family. Our families are called to be reminders of God's love for us. Schools, at their best, are caring communities that promote learning. As we grow older, we join other communities, many by choice. From sports teams, to clubs, to friends, to Church, we surround ourselves with other individuals and groups of people in communities that can reflect God's love.

Ideally, communities bring out the best in us. Within communities we can find many moments of grace. They help us accept God's grace and live our faith. And in accepting others and helping them become the best persons they can be, we affirm the dignity and equality with which we are all created. But because they are made up of imperfect people like ourselves, communities are not always healthy and do not always bring us closer to God. Our challenge is to choose communities that are life-giving or to work to change those that are not.

Reflect on ways that you are involved in communities. Share your thoughts with your Faith Partner.

FAiTH PARTNERSHiP

WRAP UP

- We are body and spirit, created in God's image, all equal in God's eyes.

- All human life has dignity because it comes from God.

- Faith is our free response to God. Grace is God's life in us. Both are gifts from God.

- We are created for community as a reflection of the communion of the Trinity.

What questions do you have about the content of this chapter?

_____

_____

_____

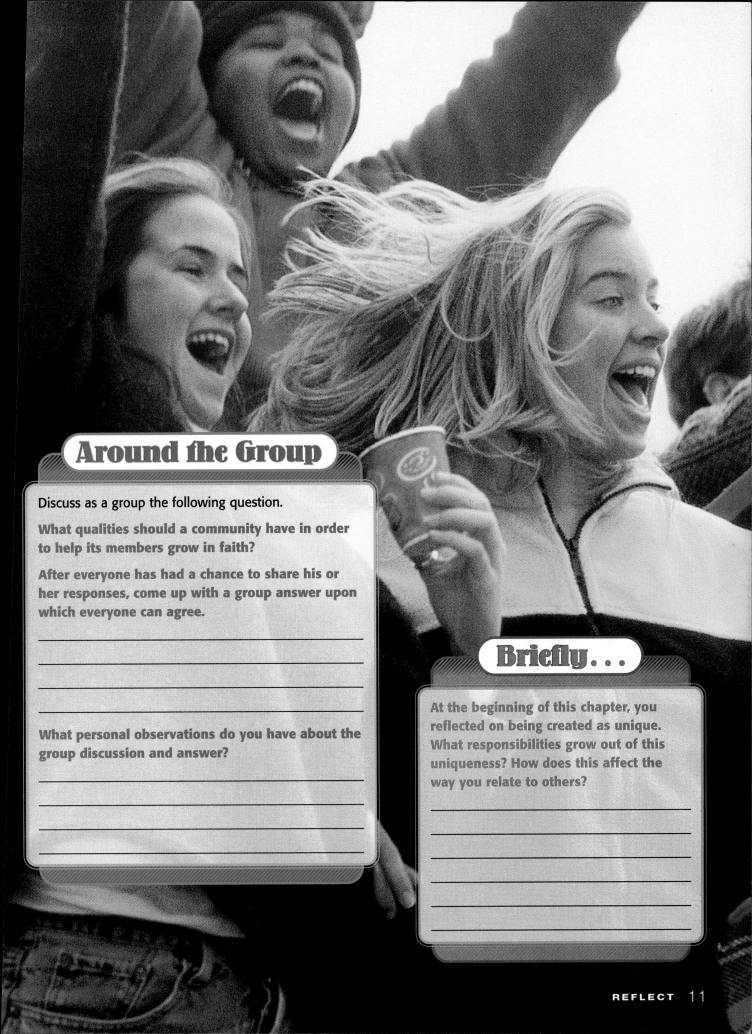

Around the Group

Discuss as a group the following question.

What qualities should a community have in order to help its members grow in faith?

After everyone has had a chance to share his or her responses, come up with a group answer upon which everyone can agree.

_____

_____

_____

_____

What personal observations do you have about the group discussion and answer?

_____

_____

_____

_____

Briefly...

At the beginning of this chapter, you reflected on being created as unique. What responsibilities grow out of this uniqueness? How does this affect the way you relate to others?

_____

_____

_____

_____

_____

_____

Goal Setting

Expressions of Faith—

We are all made in God's image and we are all part of God's family. Our lives, our abilities, and our talents are all gifts from God.

Goal setting is about reaching the potential God gave us and using our abilities to help others recognize and reach their potential. In doing so we can help build stronger, life-giving communities.

Scripture

Therefore it says,
  "Sleeper, awake!
    Rise from the dead,
    and Christ will shine on you."
Be careful then how you live, not as unwise people but as wise, making the most of the time, because the days are evil. So do not be foolish but understand what the will of the Lord is. Do not get drunk with wine, for that is debauchery; but be filled with the Spirit. . . .
Ephesians 5:14–18

20th Sunday of Ordinary Time, Cycle B

Think About It—

Setting goals starts with looking at the future and deciding who you want to be, what you want to accomplish, and how you hope to accomplish those things.

○ **What do you see yourself doing in five years? Ten years? Twenty years?**

_____

_____

_____

○ **What kind of person are you now? What kind of person do you want to be as an adult?**

_____

_____

_____

_____

○ **What are some concrete things you can do to reach those goals?**

_____

_____

_____

_____

Skill Steps-

There are different kinds of goals. Some goals focus on what we want for our outer, or social, life—such as getting good grades and having meaningful friendships. Some goals focus on what we want for our inner, or emotional, life—such as how to handle stress, sadness, anger, or fear. Some goals focus on our religious life—such as how to improve our relationship with God and how to best express our faith.

When setting goals, ask yourself the following questions:

WHO can help me? We live in communities and can rely on others. Ask a trusted adult or ask a friend to brainstorm ideas with you. Can your teacher recommend a good book or article?

WHAT will it demand of me? Are you already too busy? Should you take the goal in smaller steps? Or does this goal not challenge you enough? We must be honest about the effort needed to reach the goal.

WHY should I pursue this? Be honest with yourself on this one. We must discover our true motives and determine how much our goal will benefit others as well as ourselves.

Check It Out-

Most of my goals are
◯ social
◯ emotional
◯ spiritual

Most of my goals are
◯ easy
◯ realistic
◯ difficult to achieve
◯ almost impossible

Most of the time I ask (check as many as apply)
◯ Who can help me?
◯ What will it demand from me?
◯ Why pursue it?
◯ Who else will this benefit?
◯ How can I be open to the guidance of the Spirit?

Which of the goal-setting steps are new to you?

_____

_____

_____

Closing Prayer-

Generous God, you have created me in your image. I am a unique combination of gifts and talents, and I am united to others in your love. Help me use my abilities to glorify you and help others.

CHAPTER 2

Teachings from Scripture

"*For nothing will be impossible with God.*"
Luke 1:37

Lord Jesus, you have fulfilled the covenant your Father made with us. By your life and your sacrifice on the cross, may we have eternal life in God. Help us turn to Scripture for guidance in following your loving example. Amen.

How do you use Scripture in your life? Circle all the ways that apply.

for prayer　　*for wisdom*　　*I don't*

for discussion　　*for its challenges*

for comfort　　*at Mass*　　*for answers*

How do you think your faith would be different without the Bible?

_____

_____

_____

_____

God's
Written Word

Imagine attending school without using the written word—no books, no notes, no computers. Your backpack would certainly be lighter! But can you picture learning algebra without examples or understanding history without a written record of dates and events? School would become very difficult very quickly.

The same concept is true of our faith. The written word is an important part of passing on our faith tradition from generation to generation. The early Church passed on Jesus' teachings by word of mouth and through inspired writings. The Church realized that writing down his teachings was vital if Christianity were to survive.

Today, the wisdom found in Scripture still has meaning for us. In our search for ways to meet life's challenges, Scripture is a light that guides us.

"BLESSED ARE THE PURE IN HEART: FOR THEY WILL SEE GOD."
MATT. 5:8

Our Relationship with God

God's relationship with humanity has been marked by promises. After the sin of our first parents, God promised salvation, which he later fulfilled in his Son. God promised Abraham descendants that would number as the stars in the skies. And he promised Moses that he would deliver the Israelites from slavery in Egypt. In a loving relationship, both members give and receive. But what could humans promise God? What could humans give back to God who has no need?

After he freed the Israelites from slavery, God told Moses how the people should live in response to his promises. God gave Moses the Law, including the **Ten Commandments,** which listed the strict moral law that Moses and his people were to follow. If they lived by his commandments, which meant respecting God and their neighbors, God would protect and provide for them.

Catholics Believe

We need to interpret the Ten Commandments in light of the law of love. See Catechism, #2055.

Which of the commandments do you believe is most often broken or ignored in today's culture?

_____

_____

_____

Share your responses and thoughts with your Faith Partner.

1. I am the LORD your God. You shall not have strange gods before me.

2. You shall not take the name of the LORD your God in vain.

3. Remember to keep holy the LORD'S day.

Our Salvation

Moses and other Old Testament leaders used God's Law in their teachings. Jesus taught using himself as the example. He showed compassion for all types of people, even those whom society outcast. Through his healings, as with the leper, and through his understanding for those whose sins made them "less" in the eyes of others, as with the adulteress, Jesus shows us that all people deserve love.

Jesus, alone, lived God's Law to the fullest. In fact, we believe that Jesus fulfilled the Law and the promises of God so completely that he became our salvation. And because Jesus lived out the Law of Moses and the law of love, which summarizes the Law of Moses, he took upon himself the punishment for all of us who sin. By sacrificing his life for us, he redeemed us. By dying on the cross, Jesus gained for us eternal life. Jesus is our Savior because he so completely lived what he taught—love of God and neighbor.

Despite our best efforts and intentions, there are times when we fail to live as Jesus taught, times when we sin. But Jesus explained that although we sometimes lose our way, we are to strive to live with God the Father and with others in mind. We are to live responsibly and lovingly.

Media Message

CHRISTIAN MUSIC Many times we are told that the media is bad, full of negative images and characters. Indeed, one can find such images throughout all kinds of media, from television to music to movies. But there are many positive images and life-giving messages as well, especially with the growth of Christian contemporary music.

What music groups or artists do you know help spread the gospel? What are some of the messages?

_____
_____
_____
_____
_____
_____
_____

4. Honor your father and your mother.

5. You shall not kill.

6. You shall not commit adultery.

7. You shall not steal.

8. You shall not bear false witness against your neighbor.

9. You shall not covet your neighbor's wife.

10. You shall not covet your neighbor's goods.

(See Exodus 20:2-17.)

The Beatitudes

Jesus spent his ministry on earth announcing the good news, reminding us of God's command to love, and doing good. When asked which of God's commandments was the most important, Jesus replied that we must love God with our whole being and love our neighbor as ourselves. He added that the whole Law and all of the teachings of the prophets are based on this teaching. (See *Matthew 22:37–40.*)

As Jesus traveled around Galilee, his fame and the crowds that followed him continued to grow. At one particular place, the Gospel according to Matthew recounts, there were such large numbers of people that Jesus went up on a mountainside and began preaching so that everyone gathered could hear him. This Sermon on the Mount, as it has come to be known, covers some of Jesus' most important and influential teachings. Included in the sermon are the **Beatitudes,** teachings which sum up the way to live in God's kingdom.

Jesus also warned that it wasn't enough for us to live our *own* lives by these examples. Instead, each of us is called to change those situations that don't agree with what we know God wants us to do. For example, if a government has created laws that permit acts of violence, such as abortion, the citizens are called to work to change those laws.

Our Christian Journey

Where Did We Get the Bible? The Bible is not just one book, but many books, written over hundreds of years. The earliest parts of the Old Testament were written about 1,100 years before the birth of Jesus. The last books of the Old Testament were written by about 100 B.C. The New Testament was written between approximately A.D. 50 and 125. The collection of Scripture as Catholics know it has been recognized since at least the Council of Rome in A.D. 382. During the Protestant Reformation the Scriptures were critiqued, and since that time, Protestants have dropped from their version of the Bible some Old Testament books that were written in Greek rather than Hebrew, now known by them as the *Apocrypha.* Catholic versions of the Bible include the books of Sirach, Wisdom, Tobit, Baruch, Judith, 1 and 2 Maccabees, and some additions within the books of Esther and Daniel, while Protestant versions ordinarily do not.

For further information: Choose a book from Scripture and research its history. When was it written? Is the author known?

Our Way of **Life**

Blessed are the poor in spirit.
The kingdom of God is theirs.

Blessed are those who mourn.
They will be comforted.

Blessed are the meek.
They will inherit the earth.

Blessed are those who hunger and thirst for what is right.
They will be filled.

Blessed are those who are merciful.
They will receive mercy.

Blessed are the pure in heart.
They will see God.

Blessed are the peacemakers.
They will be called children of God.

Blessed are the oppressed for righteousness' sake.
The kingdom of God is theirs.

Blessed are you when others persecute you and speak all kinds of evil against you because of me. Rejoice and be glad. Your reward will be great in heaven.
(See Matthew 5:3–11.)

The teachings of Jesus are more than just lists of things we can or cannot do. They illustrate a way of life based on love. We can use them as a basis to judge our own lives—to see our **virtues** and **vices** more clearly.

Virtues are habits that bring us closer to God and others. The theological virtues of faith, hope, and love are gifts from God that help us in our relationship with him. If someone lives a life filled with faith, he or she is not going to stray from the ideals set by the first commandment. The cardinal virtues—prudence, fortitude, temperance, and justice—are habits we develop that help us make good decisions in our relationships with others. When a person practices justice, he or she is being a peacemaker. Living a virtuous life means we obey and respect the Law and follow Jesus' teachings.

Vices are bad habits or practices that lead us away from God and others. Sometimes a vice is failure to practice a particular virtue. For example, if someone was being bullied, he or she might need help. If an onlooker does not help, he or she neglects to act on the virtue of fortitude.

Our challenge as followers of Jesus is to live virtuously, avoiding the vices that damage our relationships. By using Scripture, we learn how God is calling us to live and respond.

Opening the Word

6th Sunday of Easter, Cycle B

If you keep my commandments, you will abide in my love, just as I have kept my Father's commandments and abide in his love. I have said these things to you so that my joy may be in you, and that your joy may be complete. John 15:10–11

Read *John 15* as well as *Matthew 5:17–20* and *1 John 2:3–17*. What do these passages tell us about God's law of love?

_____

_____

Blueprint for **Action**

Perhaps you've seen construction workers erecting a skyscraper or building houses in a new subdivision. It is amazing how they can turn concrete, steel, and wood into an office building or a house. But some of the most important work on these buildings happens long before the workers ever put hammer to nail. Designers and architects must first create the blueprints to guide the carpenters and steel workers. Blueprints are precise plans, with measurements and dimensions down to the smallest detail. The plans must be followed to the letter if the building is to be completed correctly. Even a small miscalculation or mistake can lead to big problems later on, because every step of the building process builds upon the last.

Scripture is like a blueprint for our lives. Through the Law, the prophets, the life of Jesus, and the teachings of the apostles, we get a good picture of how we are to live our lives. The Gospels, in particular, help us see how we are to follow Jesus. The life of Jesus calls us to reflect on how our lives measure up to his. The completeness with which he lived the law of love sets an example for us to follow. As we live our lives, we can look to the Scriptures to see whether our words, thoughts, and actions are leading us away from God or toward eternal life with him.

Reflect on how your life compares with the life we are all called to lead. Share your thoughts with your Faith Partner.

FaiTH PartNeRSHiP

WRAP UP

- Scripture is a light that guides us.
- Jesus made clear for us the greatest of God's commandments.
- Christians believe that Jesus fulfilled the Law.
- The Beatitudes help us live as God intended.
- Jesus is the source of salvation; his life and teachings are perfect examples of virtue.

What questions do you have about the content of this chapter?

_____

_____

_____

Around the Group

Discuss the following questions as a group.

What does it mean to love your neighbor as yourself?

Which of the Beatitudes is the most challenging and why?

After everyone has had a chance to share his or her responses to the second question, come up with a group answer upon which everyone can agree.

_____

_____

_____

_____

What personal observations do you have about the group discussion and answer?

_____

_____

_____

_____

Briefly...

At the beginning of this chapter, you reflected on Scripture in _your_ life. What would life be like if everyone followed the commandments and the teachings of Jesus?

_____

_____

_____

Share your responses and thoughts with your Faith Partner.

FaiTH PaRTNeRSHiP

Goal Setting

Expressions of Faith-

God's word helps guide our lives. It also helps us as we set goals for our lives. Jesus' teachings are the basis for goals that strengthen our relationship with God and with others. Here we will see how to set goals based on God's word.

Scripture

Teach me good judgment and knowledge, for I believe in your commandments.
Psalm 119:66

Skill Steps-

When setting goals, we must ask ourselves the following questions: *WHO can help me? WHAT will it demand of me? WHY should I pursue this?*

● Asking for God's guidance will open you up to wisdom; accepting assistance from others can also help you reach your goal.

● Be honest about the amount of effort, time, energy, and skill you will need to complete a goal.

● Check your motives. Will this goal benefit others?

Skill Builder-

Look again at the Beatitudes found earlier in this chapter. Read over the list carefully, and try to understand each one as best you can. Choose one that has special meaning for you and make it a "Be-Attitude," a goal for yourself.

Beatitude: _____

○ Who or what in your life can help you achieve this goal?

_____

_____

○ What will be demanded of you in order to achieve this goal?

_____

_____

○ Why should you pursue this goal?

_____

_____

Putting It into Practice-

Now begin practicing your own goal setting.

Write two or three personal goals.

_____

_____

For each goal, ask yourself whether the goal deals with your outer, or social, life; your inner, or emotional, life; or your religious life.

Now pick one of these goals, and reflect on the three questions in the *Skill Steps.*

⦿ WHO can help you?

_____

_____

_____

⦿ WHAT will it demand?

_____

_____

_____

⦿ WHY should you pursue this goal?

_____

_____

_____

If you have time, do this same process for your other goals. Remember the more you practice, the better you will get.

Which of the above steps for setting goals is the most difficult to answer? What can you do to make this step a natural part of your goal setting?

_____

_____

_____

Closing Prayer-

Loving God, in your wisdom and unfailing love, you gave us your word to act as a blueprint for our lives. Help us, through the grace of the Holy Spirit, to keep your commandments and follow the example of Christ, who is your word among us. In Jesus' name we pray. Amen.

Freedom, Responsibility, and Conscience

God our Father, you have given us the gift of free will. Holy Spirit, you give us the wisdom and courage to make good choices for our lives. Jesus, you saved us and set before us the example to follow. Help us live a good and just life. Amen.

A Branch Followed Is A Branch Missed. You Have The Freedom To Choose Your Path For Life ~

John Hoffman 85

Brainstorm two lists. Within the circle on the left, write areas in your life in which you have a great deal of freedom. Within the circle on the right, write areas in your life in which you have very little freedom.

_____   _____
_____   _____
_____   _____
_____   _____
_____   _____

Is it possible to have too much freedom? Explain.

_____
_____
_____

Freedom

You may remember childhood as being easy and carefree. It's easy to forget that children have very little freedom. For example, as an infant, you made no decisions for yourself. As a young child you gained some freedom but were still limited in the amount and the types of decisions you could make.

The more you mature, the more freedom you will gain. For example, you have more freedom today than you did just a few years ago. Now you have the chance to express yourself through your choice of clothes and music. You have more freedom to do things with your friends.

In the future, you will gain even more freedom. Soon, you'll be driving yourself where you want to go. You'll even choose some of your classes in school.

With so much happening in so little time, all that freedom can be difficult. Suddenly you are faced with choices you may find tough—choices about honesty, relationships, your body. It is important to take the time to make good, life-giving choices and to take responsibility for those choices. Real freedom is responsible freedom. In this sense responsibility increases freedom. Irresponsible use of freedom is actually less freedom and destruction of freedom.

Responsibility

In the first chapter, you learned that the unity of the body and soul is what makes us truly human. As humans we have the power to choose right or wrong, good or evil. We call that power **free will** and it is a gift from God. Free will means that our lives are not ruled by fate or chance. Our lives are all about choices. No other creature on earth possesses the same kind of ability to make choices. Free will is part of what it means to be created in God's image.

But having freedom does not give us the right to do or say anything and everything we please. We must recognize that some actions are right and others are wrong. We know it is wrong, for example, to yell "Fire!" in a crowded room unless there is a fire. It is also wrong to gossip or to lie. On the other hand, we know it is right to be truthful and it is good to be respectful of our adult family members.

As we read in the last chapter, we have a blueprint to help us make our choices. Through Scripture and the life of Jesus, we can discover much about what is right and what is wrong. We can know that through the moral law, we are urged to do those things that are good and to avoid those things that are evil. As followers of Jesus, we are called to strengthen our sense of **morality,** our knowledge of how to put our beliefs into action for good.

Our responsibility to the moral law increases as we grow. The more freedom we have, the more responsibility we have. As Jesus reminds us in the parable of the talents, the more we are given, the more is expected of us. (See *Matthew 25:14–30.*) And so as our freedom grows, so does our obligation to use our free will to do what is right and to become the best persons we can be. With the freedom to choose the music we listen to, for example, comes the responsibility to choose music with appropriate lyrics. We are called to choose music that shows respect for God and others.

As we become adults, we find that our choices affect more people. And so the key is to develop good patterns of behavior now. The better you are at making the right moral choices, the more joyful your life will be. You will be a person of principle, at peace with yourself, God, and others.

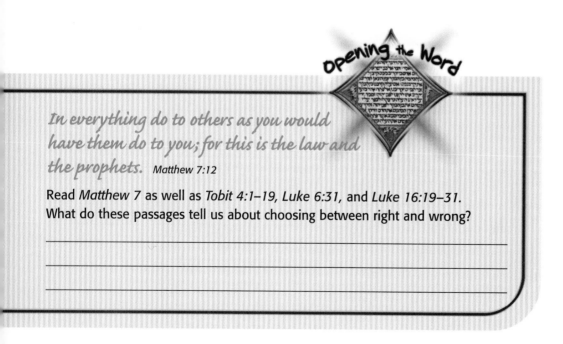

Opening the Word

In everything do to others as you would have them do to you; for this is the law and the prophets. Matthew 7:12

Read *Matthew 7* as well as *Tobit 4:1–19, Luke 6:31,* and *Luke 16:19–31.*
What do these passages tell us about choosing between right and wrong?

_____

_____

_____

Learning from Our Elders

In some cultures elder members are revered and hold special social positions within their society. In such communities the exchange of this wisdom and knowledge is an integral part of the process of growing up. Sometimes a special ceremony links a younger person with an elder so they can dialogue. In Native American cultures some elders hold story sessions in which they pass on cultural traditions as well as life knowledge. Whatever the means used, people of many cultures actively seek out wisdom from their elders. This can be a meaningful act both within the society and the lives of young people.

Share with your Faith Partner some of your family and cultural traditions. How do these traditions contribute to your life?

FaiTH PaRTNeRSHiP

Conscience

The first step in the process of making moral choices is forming an upright and truthful **conscience.** Along with reason and free will, conscience is also a gift from God, a gift that helps us know the difference between right and wrong. Freedom without conscience leads to poor choices and even sin. We are called to develop a conscience. A person who is forming an upright conscience uses his or her reason to make good decisions and tries to understand what God is guiding him or her to. In order for that to happen, we must inform, or educate, our conscience. Thankfully, besides giving us our conscience, God also gives us what we need to develop our conscience. Scripture is a light for our way. We are also helped by the power of the Holy Spirit, the advice and guidance of others whom we trust, and the teachings of the Church.

The growth of our freedom and responsibility is lifelong and so should be the education of our conscience. By wisely educating our conscience, we can grow in virtue and we can learn to control things like fear, selfishness, and pride. A strong conscience helps us overcome our weaknesses and withstand pressures from others to do wrong. The key is to actually listen to our conscience. We are faced with moral decisions every day. A choice that some might consider easy could be difficult for others. A self-confident person might easily resist the urge to join in name-calling or belittling someone else, while one less secure might be afraid to stand up to the crowd! Our job is to evaluate the decision with an educated conscience so we can act with the assurance we are making the right choice.

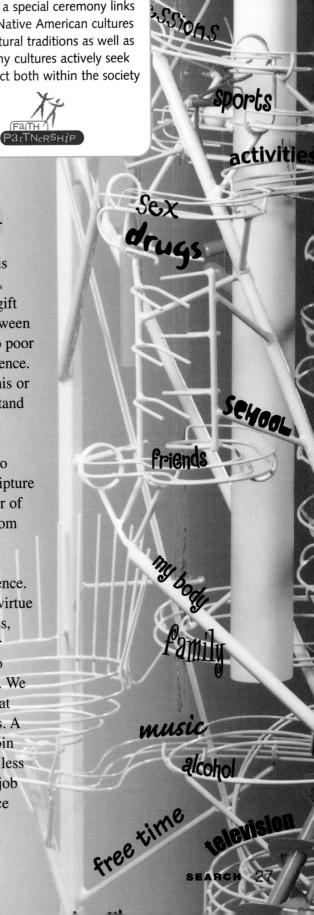

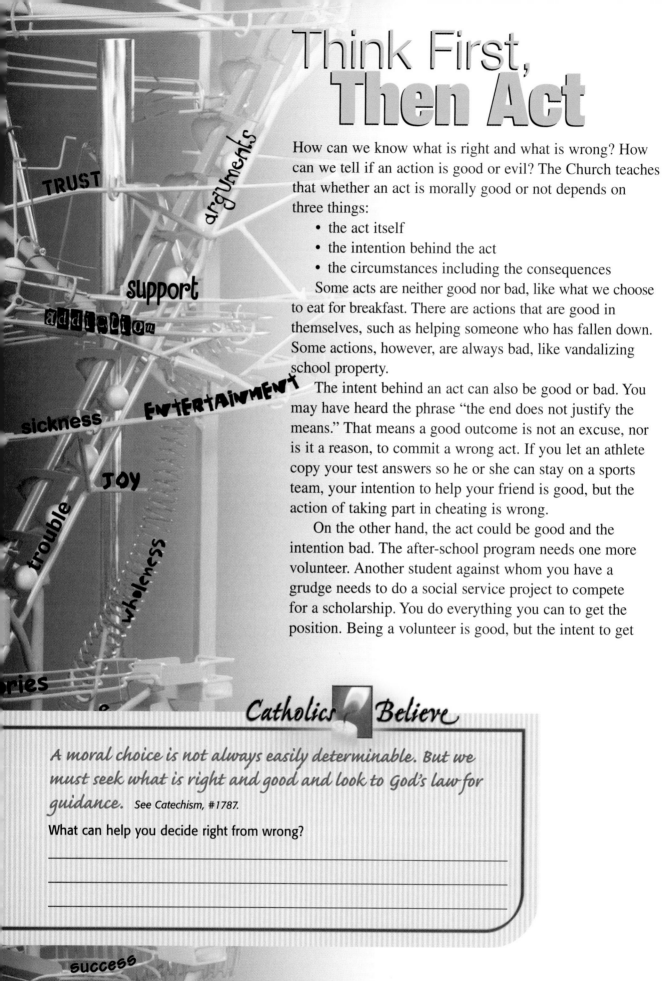

Think First, Then Act

How can we know what is right and what is wrong? How can we tell if an action is good or evil? The Church teaches that whether an act is morally good or not depends on three things:

- the act itself
- the intention behind the act
- the circumstances including the consequences

Some acts are neither good nor bad, like what we choose to eat for breakfast. There are actions that are good in themselves, such as helping someone who has fallen down. Some actions, however, are always bad, like vandalizing school property.

The intent behind an act can also be good or bad. You may have heard the phrase "the end does not justify the means." That means a good outcome is not an excuse, nor is it a reason, to commit a wrong act. If you let an athlete copy your test answers so he or she can stay on a sports team, your intention to help your friend is good, but the action of taking part in cheating is wrong.

On the other hand, the act could be good and the intention bad. The after-school program needs one more volunteer. Another student against whom you have a grudge needs to do a social service project to compete for a scholarship. You do everything you can to get the position. Being a volunteer is good, but the intent to get

Catholics Believe

A moral choice is not always easily determinable. But we must seek what is right and good and look to God's law for guidance. See Catechism, #1787.

What can help you decide right from wrong?

_____

_____

_____

revenge is bad. A good act can be less good or more good by the circumstances surrounding it. An evil act can be less evil or more evil depending on the circumstances. Telling the truth is good but is made less good if it causes harm to another. For example, if a classmate is looking for another classmate in order to beat him or her up, telling the truth about where the person is would be wrong. Stealing is always bad but taking the lunch of a student who is poor is even worse than taking it from a student who has lots of money and can easily pay for a lunch.

Every action, whether good or bad, has **consequences.** There are always physical, emotional, or spiritual results to a choice. For example, sometimes several members of a class can group together and be very cruel toward other classmates. Consequences could include disruption in learning, hurt feelings, angry retaliation, and trauma to the point of consideration of suicide. Being aware of consequences requires us to think ahead, put ourselves in another's shoes, and consider what might happen as a result of our choices.

Our Christian Journey

Despite the Consequences Sometimes, doing the right thing comes with a high price. The life of Thomas More is a good example. Born in England, Thomas was the son of a lawyer and judge. By the time he was in his thirties, Thomas had become one of the leading scholars and thinkers of the time. He wrote poetry, history, prayers, and books on religion. He even tutored the future King Henry VIII of England.

When Henry became king, Thomas was appointed Lord Chancellor, the king's highest assistant. But when Henry desired to divorce his first wife Catherine, Thomas was concerned because Henry's reasons for wanting the annulment were political. Thomas refused to sign a letter to the pope, requesting the annulment. Soon afterward, Thomas was forced to resign his position. After Thomas refused to sign the Act of Supremacy, a document stating that the pope no longer had authority over the Church of England, he was charged with treason and was beheaded. The feast day of Saint Thomas More is June 22.

For further information: Read or watch a video of the play "A Man for All Seasons" for more insight into the life of Saint Thomas More.

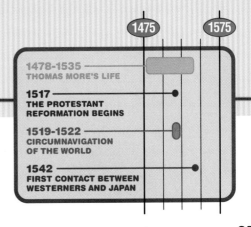

1475	1575

1478-1535
THOMAS MORE'S LIFE

1517
THE PROTESTANT
REFORMATION BEGINS

1519-1522
CIRCUMNAVIGATION
OF THE WORLD

1542
FIRST CONTACT BETWEEN
WESTERNERS AND JAPAN

Responsibility and Consequences

Having free will means that we have the ability to choose our actions. And we are responsible for the results, or consequences, of our actions. As we learned in this chapter, we need to take these consequences into consideration when we make moral decisions. Remember, though, that not only do consequences affect others, they also affect us.

Perhaps you helped someone study for a difficult exam. That person may get a better grade and have a better understanding of the subject due to your help. But you also receive something as a result of your good deed. There is a joy to working with someone to accomplish something. There is comfort in knowing that someone needs something that you can provide. And there is warmth in a relationship when people can rely on and help each other.

Think of the movie *It's a Wonderful Life.* George, the main character, is made to see what the lives of his family and friends would be like if not for his actions. Your life is the same way. Perhaps you are the only person your sibling can talk to openly. Or maybe your best friend understands percentages only the way you present it. Whatever gifts you have for others, share it. You will gain as much as others do.

Reflect on being responsible for the consequences of our actions. Share your thoughts with your Faith Partner.

FAITH PARTNERSHIP

WRAP UP

- We have been created with the freedom to choose our own actions, but we are called to make responsible choices.
- Choosing to live morally is the way to true freedom.
- Conscience is a gift from God that helps us know the difference between right and wrong and choose what is right.
- Conscience formation is a lifelong process.

What questions do you have about the content of this chapter?

_____

_____

_____

Around the Group

Discuss the following questions as a group.

When one makes good moral choices based on the commandments, Beatitudes, and teaching of the Church from what is a person freed? For what is a person freed?

After everyone has had a chance to share his or her responses, come up with a group answer upon which everyone can agree.

_____

_____

_____

_____

What personal observations do you have about the group discussion and answer?

_____

_____

_____

_____

Briefly...

At the beginning of this chapter, you thought about freedom in your life. How does irresponsibility produce false freedom or lesson freedom?

_____

_____

_____

SKILLS for Christian Living

Forming a Conscience

Expressions of Faith-

We have the freedom to make our own choices, but we also have the responsibility to make good decisions. Forming and educating your conscience and making right choices is one way for you to respond to God's love.

Forming a conscience, then, is not just something we do to grow closer to God and to others. It is something we do to make our life better.

Scripture

My child, keep my words
and store up my commandments with you;
keep my commandments and live,
keep my teachings as the apple of your eye;
bind them on your fingers,
write them on the tablet of your heart.
Say to wisdom, "You are my sister,"
and call insight your intimate friend. . . .

Proverbs 7:1–4

Think About It-

Education of the conscience is a lifelong process that begins with actively seeking wisdom and truth for understanding right and wrong. If you were to form your conscience about the following topics, where would you go for information? What would help you make a good decision regarding these issues?

Issues	Where to Look for Information
Underage drinking	_____ _____ _____
Buying music with lyrics that glorify violence	_____ _____ _____
Exploring an inappropriate Web site	_____ _____ _____

Skill Steps-

In order to develop an informed conscience, we must first search for wisdom. It will act as our compass, guiding us through life, helping us evaluate different life situations. For Catholics there are four basic sources of wisdom: (1) the Bible, (2) the teachings of the Catholic Church, (3) science, or sources of physical proven fact, and (4) the community. Sometimes all four sources agree. Sometimes they do not. Sometimes the wisdom of the community goes against the other three sources of wisdom. For example, the fact that an action is legal, does not mean it is right. For further help we can do the following: (1) remember that God wants us to form a good conscience; (2) know that God wants us to trust the wisdom of the Church and Scripture beyond science or the community; and (3) pray for the guidance of the Holy Spirit.

Check It Out-

Reflect on your efforts to form your conscience. On a scale from 1 to 10, rate each of the statements below. (With 1 meaning always and 10 meaning never.)

_____ I read the newspaper or listen to or watch the news regarding current events and moral issues.

_____ I read the Bible on my own to become familiar with God's word.

_____ I talk with adults about current events and moral issues.

_____ I ask questions about current events and moral issues.

_____ I seek out the Church's teachings on moral issues.

_____ I seek wisdom by taking time and making an effort to identify moral issues and situations I face in my life.

_____ I spend time with God in prayer when I am making a decision regarding what is right.

Overall, where are *you* on the "forming your conscience" scale? Rate yourself from 1 to 10. (With 1 being lowest and 10 being highest.) _____

Closing Prayer-

*Loving God our Father, you have given us all we need to **seek** you in this life and to be with you eternally. May your Holy Spirit **guide** us in our search for wisdom and may we follow the teachings of your Son, Jesus. Help us see that **true freedom** comes in hearing and following you. We ask this in Jesus' name. Amen.*

CHAPTER 4

Those
Who Guide Us

Spirit of God, send your blessings upon your people. May the things we attempt to do be completed with the gift of your wisdom, and may we end our journey face to face with you. Amen.

On a scale from 1 to 9, rank the following sources in their importance to your growth as a person. (1 should represent most important; 9 the least important.)

_____ books   _____ prayer   _____ the Internet

_____ friends   _____ family   _____ TV programs

_____ teachers   _____ other adults   _____ Church community

Which sources seemed harder to rank than others? Did you want to place some sources together at the same rank? Explain your answers.

_____

_____

_____

_____

_____

Freedom Has
Limits

There are many limits on our freedom. Some of those limits are violations of human dignity, but many are intended to promote safety and respect for others. From groups of friends to groups of nations, there are limitations that are really guidelines for how we are expected to live for our own good and the good of others. In a sense they don't limit our freedom but help us realize it properly.

As people with free will, we need to realize that one of our community duties is to understand and follow the guidelines set by the community. But our communities also have a responsibility. They should set and maintain guidelines that help community members grow and live together.

The Family as
Domestic Church

We have already seen how God's word, the Scriptures, helps us follow his Law and form our conscience. God also places in our lives people with **authority,** the power and responsibility to lead others. Ideally, people in authority will lead us to God.

The first people God puts in our lives are our families. From the moment of a child's conception, parents are responsible for guiding their children. Parenting is a huge job. Meeting their own physical, emotional, and spiritual needs is tough enough; but parents must also meet the needs of their children.

Meeting physical needs for things like food, clothing, and shelter is something families do according to their means. These are basic requirements for human life to which every human is entitled. Throughout the Gospels we read that Jesus took care of people's needs both physical and spiritual.

Opening the Word

Children, obey your parents in the Lord, for this is right. "Honor your father and mother"— this is the first commandment with a promise: "so that it may be well with you and you may live long on the earth."

And, fathers, do not provoke your children to anger, but bring them up in the discipline and instruction of the Lord.

Ephesians 6:1–4

Read *Ephesians 6* as well as *Exodus 20:12, Proverbs 23:22,* and *Colossians 3:20–21.* What do these passages tell about the relationship between family members?

_____

_____

_____

Godparents share in the responsibility to raise a child in the Catholic faith.

And so parents must provide for the physical and spiritual needs of the children. It is adult family members who must be the first teachers for their children in faith, prayer, and the virtues. The family must also provide moral guidance. Adult family members who bring harm to children sin against them and against God.

The Christian family is called to be the **domestic Church,** a community of faith, hope, and charity. Part of providing moral guidance is to encourage children to grow in their talents and gifts and to help them realize that the first calling of the Christian is to follow Jesus. With this duty adult family members should respect and encourage their children in their vocations, or calling in life.

Children also have duties. From the very beginnings of our faith history, children have been called to respect the God-given authority of their parents. God has put parents and other adult family members in our lives to help us grow closer to him. He has given these family members authority to teach us the faith. And so we owe them respect, because their authority comes from God. And we owe them gratitude for the sacrifices they make for us.

We also need to help with younger brothers and sisters. For them, we can be authority figures and role models, guiding them closer to God. Respect and honor can ripple throughout the family. Indeed, one of the most important keys to family harmony is the respect family members show each other.

Rite Response

The Role of the Family

The Church takes the relationship between family and faith very seriously. In the Sacrament of Baptism, parents and godparents are reminded of their responsibilities. The priest or deacon states that the parents and godparents are promising to train the child in the practice of the faith. It will be their duty to bring him or her up to keep God's commandments as Christ taught and to love God and their neighbor. Parents and godparents are directed to make it their "constant care" to bring up the child in the faith and to keep him or her from sin.

Catholics Believe

Living a moral life is one way to worship God. **See Catechism, #2031.**

Choose from the examples below one area that you want to begin practicing or on which you want to improve in order to worship God better. Then write how you could do this.

> talking respectfully to family members
>
> acting on lessons learned in the readings at Mass
>
> learning about Church teachings
>
> acting as a good guide for your siblings
>
> discussing faith questions with family, teachers, and Church leaders

_____

_____

_____

The Church
as Guide

Adult family members are our first teachers in the ways of faith, but they are not our only teachers. They receive support and encouragement from the Church. In fact, the Church, guided by the Holy Spirit, has a duty to help proclaim the gospel to each of its members. Another result of the Church's guidance from the Holy Spirit is that it has the moral authority to lead and to teach its people. The teaching authority of the Church, called the **magisterium,** includes the pope, bishops, and pastors. It is their responsibility to preach the Catholic faith to the people of God, to teach how to apply the teachings of God to daily life, and to address moral questions. The magisterium must also encourage Church members to keep the **precepts of the Church,** a list of some of the duties of Catholics. Participation in the Mass on Sundays and holy days and rest from unnecessary labor on those days is one of the precepts. The precepts of the Church help unite us with Jesus in the Eucharist, who nourishes us, giving us the strength to live the Christian life.

Society as Guide

Besides being members of our families and of the Church, we are also members of our society. Our society is set up in such a way that we give certain individuals authority to make laws and other individuals the authority to carry out or enforce laws. We have a system of lawmakers, police officers and other law enforcement agents, and courts to guide us in maintaining order and creating a just society. And each of us has a personal duty to follow the laws of society and to work to create a society in which people strive for truth, justice, unity, and freedom.

In all things we are to follow God and our consciences first. If a civil law or authority goes against God's Law, we must follow God's Law first, and then we must work to change that civil law. For example in World War II, as Adolf Hitler was exterminating the Jewish population of Europe, it was illegal to hide or protect Jews. And yet many people broke that law and risked their lives by hiding Jews in their own homes. Today some states allow capital punishment. There are Catholic bishops and many other Catholics who are working to change the laws permitting capital punishment.

Share your thoughts with your Faith Partner about laws that seem unjust to you.

FaiTH ParTNeRSHiP

Follow Me

Jesus urges us to follow him. Along the way he gives us many guides. Those people who have rightful authority in our lives—adult family members, teachers, coaches, the Church, the government—all have the ability and responsibility to help us lead a moral life. If a person in authority makes you uncomfortable or you question what the person is saying or doing in light of morals and Jesus' teaching, you should speak to another adult. All of us have two roles —followers and leaders—and we are called to do both well.

Infallibility The magisterium of the Church has many roles. Among others, it serves as both teacher and leader of the faithful. To help the magisterium, we believe that the Holy Spirit has granted the bishops in union with the pope and the pope individually the *charism,* or gift, of infallibility. Infallibility was officially defined during the First Vatican Council (1869–1870) but it has its roots in Christ's gift of the guidance of the Holy Spirit to the apostles. Infallibility means that certain Church teachings on faith and morals are free from error. This does not mean that all statements on faith and morals are infallible. Only those statements that are *ex cathedra* ("from the chair"), or are clearly intended to be infallible, are considered to be so. Since the First Vatican Council, the assumption of Mary (1950) has been declared infallible. However, whether infallible or not, any statements issued by the magisterium concerning faith and morals are intended to guide and inform our faith and require assent and obedience.

For further information: The magisterium's duty to educate and lead Church members is also assigned to the many priests and parishes within the Church community. Find out what programs your parish has to help educate its members. Is there something you would be interested in attending?

Everyone Has a Role

Everyone's family life is unique, just as every person is unique. At their most basic and practical level, families are the result of the way humans reproduce. Every one of us has parents. We can't exist without them. At their most profound and spiritual level, families are a gift from God. Families are the means God has given us for passing on the faith and for helping each person grow in love.

Some families accept that challenge. Adult family members take their responsibilities seriously and do their best to raise their children with love. Children grow in respect and faith. But some families do not accept their duty. There are adult family members who neglect their roles as loving authorities. And there are children who defy, rather than honor, their family members.

Whatever the state of a family, each member has a role. As a child in a family, you are called by God to honor and respect family members. If you have younger siblings, God calls you to be a role model, a good example for your younger brothers and sisters. You have the duty to show them what it means to grow in faith and love. If an adult, even when in authority, harms you or your siblings you have a responsibility to inform someone who can help. If you have older siblings, you are called to learn from their good example. Or maybe you are to learn from their mistakes. And finally, as a son or daughter of God, you are called to respect his authority in your life and to follow the example of your brother Jesus.

Reflect on your own family role and responsibilities. Share your thoughts with your Faith Partner.

FaiTH ParTNeRSHiP

WRAP UP

- •Members of a family have responsibilities to one another.

- •We receive our moral foundation from our families, the Church, and others with rightful authority.

- •The family, as the domestic Church, is called to instruct its members on how to live a faithful and moral life.

Circle a topic or a term in this chapter about which you would like more discussion. Write on the lines below those discussion topics.

_____

_____

_____

Around the Group

Discuss the following questions as a group.

What does it mean to be a good son or daughter?

How is family the domestic Church?

After everyone has had a chance to share his or her responses to the first question, come up with a group answer upon which everyone can agree.

_____

_____

_____

_____

What personal observations do you have about the group discussion and answer?

_____

_____

_____

_____

Briefly...

At the beginning of this chapter, you rated sources of guidance. Now after reading this chapter, what do you see as the most important guide(s) for you?

_____

_____

_____

Forming a Conscience

Expressions of Faith-

The Church, our families, and others with rightful authority provide for us the moral compass to guide us to God. We are called to honor those in authority and to exercise authority correctly ourselves. But as people with free will, we have the choice to answer those calls or not. The key to forming a conscience is to listen to those sources of wisdom as we make our decisions.

Scripture

Happy are those who find wisdom,
    and those who get understanding,
for her income is better than silver,
    and her revenue better than gold.
She is more precious than jewels,
    and nothing you desire can compare with her.

Proverbs 3:13–15

Skill Steps-

We receive guidance from four sources: (1) the Bible, (2) the teachings of the Catholic Church, (3) science or sources of physical proven fact, and (4) the community. When all four sources do not agree on an issue, follow the Church and Scripture.

- Not everyone has an informed conscience.
- God expects us to develop an informed conscience. It is a way of showing God gratitude, honor, and respect for life and freedom.
- Forming a conscience includes seeking wisdom from the above four sources.
- God provides us with rightful authorities to guide us, including our families and the Church.
- Spend time in prayer. It will help you figure out your role as both a follower of Christ and as a leader of others.

Skill Builder-

Pick one of the following topics. Write what you think each of the four sources of wisdom might say about it.

- Cloning
- Physician-assisted suicide
- War
- The Ku Klux Klan
- Scientific research using living embryos

_____
_____
_____
_____
_____
_____
_____

Putting It into Practice–

Take your reflections from the *Skill Builder* exercise and practice forming your own conscience.

1. Write a moral topic you would like to study or about which you would like to know more.

   _____

   _____

   _____

2. With what sources of wisdom do you want to become more familiar as you study this issue?

   _____

   _____

   _____

3. List any individuals you want to consult on this issue.

   _____

   _____

I called on God, and the spirit of wisdom came to me.

Wisdom 7:7

Now that you know how to form your conscience, you can notice issues in your world and begin learning about those issues. In the future this skill can help you in situations such as determining for whom you will vote in elections or whether you will work to change something in your school or community.

Continue putting this skill into practice. Into what other moral topics would you like to look?

_____

_____

_____

Closing Prayer–

*Loving Father, guide our family members to act with your justice and mercy. Jesus, you are our brother. Help us follow in your footsteps and live according to your example of **unbounded love**. Holy Spirit, you guide our family and our Church. Bless those who lead us with wisdom and love and help us be open to their guidance. Amen.*

CHAPTER

5

Loving Father, you have given us the gift of free will. Jesus, our Redeemer, you gave your life to save us. Holy Spirit, source of our strength, help us recognize our sins and seek your guidance. Amen.

Sin *and* Separation

Answer the following questions.

What is sin?

_____

_____

_____

Can you sin without knowing it?

_____

_____

_____

Is it more sinful to take money from your mom's purse or from the Sunday collection at Mass?

_____

_____

_____

Choices

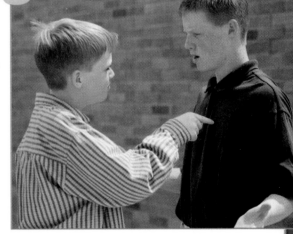

At some point in our lives, we've all sinned. We may not have intended to cause harm or hurt, but we knowingly chose to act in a sinful way. We may have lied to keep a friend from getting into trouble with the teacher, or maybe we glanced at a classmate's paper during a test. Whatever the situation, we intentionally made a wrong choice, and we sinned.

Because of free will, we can choose our actions. But sometimes curiosity, emotions, or our friends may cloud our judgment. And when this happens, we may make an incorrect choice. Sometimes an incorrect choice is a sin. When we sin, we go against God and against our relationships with others. And no matter how insignificant an action might be, it has consequences.

From the Beginning

Have you ever seen a TV sitcom in which the plot revolved around one character trying to cover up something he or she did wrong? Usually the person gets into more and more trouble by saying or doing things intended to make the wrong action seem right. The initial poor choice is followed by another, then another, creating a snowball effect. However bad the original choice may have been, the effect of continuing that choice is several times worse.

Part of what makes these shows funny is that we have faced similar situations. We know what it is like to do something wrong and then try to avoid taking responsibility for our actions. Doing the right thing can seem so hard for us, especially when doing the wrong thing looks so easy. We may even tell ourselves that we will benefit from the wrong choice. But in the end we have to face the consequences of our actions.

Sin is a deliberate wrong choice to do something contrary to God's law. We may believe a sinful act is best for us at the time. Or we may think there is no victim. But if we look more closely, we can see that these choices really separate us from those around us. The lies sometimes used to cover up a sinful choice do not protect us; instead, they tell others that we are capable of lying and that we cannot be trusted.

opening the Word

1st Sunday of Lent, Cycle A

Therefore just as one man's trespass led to condemnation for all, so one man's act of righteousness leads to justification and life for all. Romans 5:18

Read *Romans 5* as well as *Genesis 3:1–24* and *Titus 3:3–7.* Illustrate below your own interpretation of the connection between original sin and Christ's saving grace.

Role-play with your Faith Partner a situation in which a wrong choice, such as lying, leads to a string of wrong choices and consequences.

FaiTH PaRTNeRSHiP

In *Genesis 3:1–24* the writers tell a story about the beginning of sin in the world, the first humans' choice to disobey God and turn from his friendship. According to the story, the first humans compounded their sin by lying about it to God and by refusing to take responsibility for their actions. **Original sin** is the loss of original holiness and justice that resulted in the situation of alienation from God and the "sin of the world." The permanent after-effect—the inclination to choose what is wrong and turn away from God—is called **concupiscence.**

Even after celebrating the Sacraments of Baptism and Reconciliation, through which God forgives our sins, because of concupiscence we continue to struggle with **temptation,** the attraction to do what we know is wrong. Sometimes we give in to temptation and make a wrong choice.

Because of our weakened human condition and concupiscence, we can begin to think that good can result from evil deeds. But freely chosen wrong acts are sinful, no matter what we think the results may be.

OUR CHRISTIAN JOURNEY

God's Love Julian of Norwich was an English mystic who lived in a time when people were very aware of the grave consequences of their sins. In her ***Book of Showings,*** also known as the ***Revelations of Divine Love,*** she emphasized that God sees our sin and loves us still. Through her writing Julian stressed that, when we are wounded by sin and believe we are no longer worthy of love, the Holy Spirit creates in us a longing that calls us back from a state of separation and sin into relationship with God. No sin of ours can hinder God's love for us because his love is always greater than our sin.

For further information: Research on the Internet Julian's life to discover how she came to write her ***Book of Showings*** and to find out more about her thoughts on sin, God's grace, and the power of the Holy Spirit.

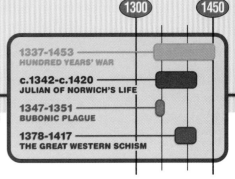

1300		1450

1337-1453
HUNDRED YEARS' WAR

c.1342-c.1420
JULIAN OF NORWICH'S LIFE

1347-1351
BUBONIC PLAGUE

1378-1417
THE GREAT WESTERN SCHISM

God calls us to recognize our sin and our need for his forgiving love.   See Catechism, #1847.

What does this statement tell us about our need to admit our sinful actions?

_____

_____

_____

Failing to **Love**

In Hebrew the word *sin* comes from a word that means "missing the mark," not measuring up to the goodness and love for which God created us. Sin can be defined as turning away from God and failing to love. Sin violates God's Law, but more important it violates the loving relationship we have with God, with others, and with our own best selves. Sin can be active (called *sin of commission*—doing what we know is wrong) or passive (called *sin of omission*—failing to do what we know is right and ought to be done). If a person deliberately destroyed or harmed another person's property, he or she would have committed an active sin. And if that person's friend stood by and watched the damage being done, the friend would have committed a sin of omission. Both of them, the actor and the observer, have made a wrong choice.

Sometimes sin is committed by an entire group of people. **Social sin** exists when a community or society denies others their rights or creates or tolerates structures of sin. Slavery and events such as the Holocaust during World War II are examples of social sin. Some would suggest the percentage of children in poverty and hunger in our country is social sin.

The seriousness, or gravity, of sin depends on certain conditions. Some sinful acts are so seriously wrong that they literally kill the love we have in our hearts. We call such gravely wrong actions **mortal sin** because we choose to break off our relationship with God, and so we experience spiritual death. For sin to be mortal, (1) it must be a grave matter (such as murder or child abuse), (2) we must know that it is seriously wrong, and (3) we must freely choose to do it anyway.

Most of our sinful actions and omissions aren't mortal sins. **Venial sin**—a less serious turning away from God's love—does not terminate our relationship with God, though it does do damage to it. A venial sin may be a freely chosen wrong, but not gravely wrong, action. Doing a grave wrong without full knowledge or without full freedom may also be a venial sin. The great danger of venial sin is that it can lead to moral sloppiness and can even make it easier to choose mortal sin.

Not Meant to Be Alone

We are created for a life connected to others and to God. It is in these relationships that we experience the life and happiness God wants for us. Sin puts a wall between us and God. It is our deeds and words that isolate us from him and others. Consider the damage done to relationships as a result of gossip and rumor. Mistrust replaces trust; fear replaces self-expression; doubt replaces love.

The pain we feel as a result of sin and separation gives us a taste of hell, or eternal separation from God. The joy we feel when we are connected to God and others suggests to us what life must be like in heaven, at one with God. Those who seek forgiveness from God receive it, while those who, to the end of their lives, choose to live a life separated from God face an eternity without him, an experience of isolation and emptiness.

Christ's death and resurrection put us in right relationship with God, but we need to ask forgiveness for our sins. God has chosen us and God continues to choose us . . . always. So no matter how many times we sin, we can always turn to God for forgiveness and know God is waiting to receive us back in mercy and love.

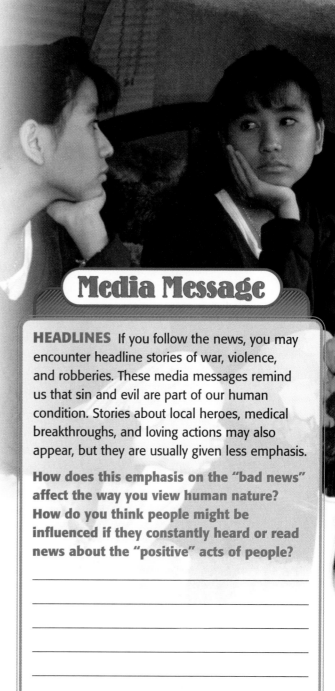

Media Message

HEADLINES If you follow the news, you may encounter headline stories of war, violence, and robberies. These media messages remind us that sin and evil are part of our human condition. Stories about local heroes, medical breakthroughs, and loving actions may also appear, but they are usually given less emphasis.

How does this emphasis on the "bad news" affect the way you view human nature? How do you think people might be influenced if they constantly heard or read news about the "positive" acts of people?

_____
_____
_____
_____
_____
_____

Focus On

Capital Sins
Vices that lead us to other sinful actions are called *capital sins,* or the seven deadly sins. The capital sins are pride, greed, envy, anger, gluttony, laziness, and lust.

The Bigger Picture

Sin is separation. It is a choice that stresses and sometimes breaks our ties with others. But we do not have to sin. By taking the time to consider the results of our choices, we can see past the sinful choice to the virtuous one.

Sometimes a lie seems to provide an easy way out of an uncomfortable situation. Maybe deciding to cheat on a test rather than study gives us a chance to do something more enjoyable. Or gossiping about another classmate makes us feel better about ourselves and helps hide personal insecurities. Whatever the sin, whatever the result, the poor choice provides only a short-term "solution."

We must look honestly into our hearts and face the problems or situations that cause us to want to sin. We must find the real issue and address it directly. For instance, cheating on one test may not seem too terrible. We might think that we would never do it again. But if we reflect on why we didn't take the time or effort to study, we might find an answer that will help us not only for the situation at hand but in the future as well. Do we need to spend less time on the telephone? Or can we turn off the television a half hour earlier?

Sin and separation do not need to happen. There is always a better way to act for our own good and for the good of our relationships with God and with others. Think about it.

Reflect on the consequences of sin and how we can work to avoid sin. Share your thoughts and any questions you have from the chapter with your Faith Partner.

FaiTH ParTNeRSHiP

WRAP UP

- Because of the effects of original sin, all of us struggle against concupiscence.
- Sin is any deliberate speech, action, desire, or omission that turns us away from God.
- Sin separates us from other people.
- Venial sin damages but does not break off our relationship with God.
- Mortal sin breaks off our relationship with God.

Which of the above do you want to discuss further?

_____

_____

_____

Around the Group

Discuss the following questions as a group.

What influences someone to make sinful choices?

Who or what can help a person resist the temptation to sin and make wise moral decisions?

After everyone has had a chance to share his or her responses to the second question, come up with a group answer upon which everyone can agree.

_____
_____
_____
_____

What personal observations do you have about the group discussion and answer?

_____
_____
_____
_____

Briefly. . .

At the beginnning of this chapter, you reflected on sin. How would you answer those questions now? Based on what you have learned, how might you best recognize a sinful action?

_____
_____
_____

Examining Conscience

Expressions of Faith-

Examining Conscience is a skill that helps us recognize whom we have hurt, the effects of our hurtful words or actions, how we might repair our relationships, and what we can do to make more virtuous choices in the future. When we examine our conscience, we ask questions about and reflect on our past actions.

Think About It-

A student spreads a sexual rumor about another classmate. Another student hears the rumor, knows it's false, but doesn't stick up for the truth. At which student would you be mad if you were the victim? (Circle one.)

Scripture

Let no evil talk come out of your mouths, but only what is useful for building up, as there is need, so that your words may give grace to those who hear. And do not grieve the Holy Spirit of God, with which you were marked with a seal for the day of redemption. Put away from you all bitterness and wrath and anger and wrangling and slander, together with all malice, and be kind to one another, tenderhearted, forgiving one another, as God in Christ has forgiven you.

Ephesians 4:29–32 | 19th Sunday of Ordinary Time, Cycle B

the student who spread the rumor

neither

both

the student who didn't stand up for the truth

We can sin by doing the wrong thing or by failing to do the right thing. Both students were wrong.

Skill Steps-

A sin is a deliberate choice we make that hurts or destroys our relationship with God, with others, or with ourselves. And we do that anytime we choose to do the wrong thing, such as stealing a CD from a store or choosing to say something negative about another person. But we also sin when we choose not to do the right thing, for example, when we don't try to prevent a friend from stealing or we don't stop another person from gossiping. We can sin when we commit and when we omit.

Examining Conscience is a skill in which we set aside some quiet time to reflect on things we have done. When we perform an examination of conscience, we don't just reflect on the sinful choices we make. We look at the whole picture. We need to be proud of our successes but be aware of the times when we may have hurt someone through a sinful act, such as lying.

When you're examining your conscience, here's an easy process to remember: ADMIT what you COMMIT and what you OMIT. By admitting that you have hurt someone, you are preparing yourself for the reconciliation process.

Check It Out-

Place a check mark next to the statements that apply to you.

◯ I try not to make selfish decisions.

◯ I work to my full potential.

◯ I think about the consequences of my decisions before I act.

◯ I'm learning to recognize when I make wrong choices.

◯ I make an effort to repair damaged relationships.

How many did you check? Based on your responses, on what kinds of things do you need to work?

_____

_____

_____

Closing Prayer-

Loving God our Father, our sinful choices damage our relationships with you and others. *Give us* the *courage* and *humility* to admit when we have sinned and the *strength* to make the virtuous choice the next time. Help us follow your son's example by **respecting** ourselves and others. We ask this in Jesus' name. Amen.

Forgiveness and Reconciliation

Loving God, like the father of the prodigal son, you welcome us with open arms. Jesus, you lead us to the Father and when we lose our way, you call us to reconciliation. Holy Spirit grant us the humility and the courage to turn toward Jesus.

What Do You Think?

Circle words, phrases, or feelings that come to mind when you think of forgiveness.

relief   grace

end of hurting   God

peace   healing

love   joy

other: _____

Which item from your list is the most important factor in your own need for forgiveness? Why?

_____
_____
_____
_____

A Second Chance

In the parable of the prodigal son, Jesus tells of the forgiving power of God. (See *Luke 15:11–32.*) When we sin, we take the gifts God has given us and we abuse them. Maybe we abuse our own bodies with unhealthy dieting or by using drugs or tobacco products. Or maybe we break trust with someone, hurt another, or exploit others. God does not condemn us for these sins. Instead, he gives us another chance. Like the father of the prodigal son, he offers us the grace to turn back to him and he waits for our return.

The parable also provides us with a model for forgiving others. Like the father in the story who was ready to forgive long before the son returned, we are called to forgive when someone asks for forgiveness. If our relationships with others reflect God's love, they are rooted in forgiveness.

Reconciliation with Others

We are social beings by nature. We need to be in relationship with others and with God. And yet, because of our weakened human nature, we have a tendency to turn away from others and God and live for ourselves alone. As a result, **reconciliation** is necessary. Very simply, reconciliation is the process of bringing together people who have been separated. When we reconcile, we experience forgiveness and make peace with each other.

There are many situations in life where reconciliation is needed. And there are many ways that we use to reconcile ourselves with others. When we were very young, we were taught to apologize as a way to make up for wrong actions. As we mature, our methods of reconciliation also need to mature. An apology can be strengthened by our attempt to make amends for any wrong done. We can say we're sorry as well as help repair the wrong we have done. For example, if we broke a neighbor's garage window while we were playing baseball with friends, we can admit to the neighbor that we broke the window and we can pay to replace the window.

Sometimes a wrong action does not involve something that can be replaced with money. If we help ruin the reputation of a classmate, money cannot fix that wrong. We can, however, work to restore his or her reputation—perhaps by admitting what we did and apologizing in the school newspaper. There may be other times when many people are involved in conflict. In these cases the group can sit down and discuss their problem openly and work toward compromise with conflict resolution.

Opening the Word

24th Sunday of Ordinary Time, Cycle A

Then Peter came and said to him, "Lord, if another member of the church sins against me, how often should I forgive? As many as seven times?" Jesus said to him, "Not seven times, but, I tell you, seventy-seven times." Matthew 18:21–22

Read *Matthew 18:21–35* as well as *Luke 5:17–26* and *John 8:3–11*. How can the act of asking for forgiveness be both difficult and comforting? How can forgiving be both difficult and comforting?

_____

_____

_____

Celebrating
Reconciliation

With God's grace we come to recognize our sinfulness and its consequences through the skill of examining our conscience. We respond to God's call to **conversion,** turning away from sin and back to God. Conversion cannot be a once-in-a-lifetime event. It is something to which we are called every time we find ourselves failing to love. The Eucharist strengthens our conversion and charity, forgives venial sin, and unites us with others in the Body of Christ.

The Church also celebrates the forgiveness of sins in the Sacrament of Reconciliation, also known as the Sacrament of Penance. The purpose of this sacrament is to reconcile us with God and the Church and to celebrate our reconciliation with those whom we have harmed. The reconciliation process within the sacrament consists of three actions by the person seeking forgiveness: contrition, confession, and penance, or satisfaction, which includes the intent to repair the wrong done.

Contrition is the deep sorrow we feel when we have sinned. This feeling also includes the resolution not to sin again.

Confession is the act of telling our sins to a priest during the Sacrament of Reconciliation. After examining our conscience, we must confess to any mortal sins we have committed.

OUR CHRISTIAN JOURNEY

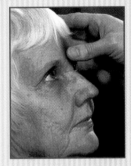

Seasons of Change
Although we are called to conversion each day, the Seasons of Advent and Lent are times in the Church year when we place special emphasis on reconciliation with God. During Advent we are called to renew the spirit of Christ within our hearts. The first two weeks of Advent focus on the second coming of Christ, while the last two weeks look toward the upcoming holy day—Christmas. This holy day commemorates Jesus' birth—the incarnation of the Son of God. During Lent we strive to deepen our relationship with God through prayer, fasting (eating less and not between meals on specific days during the season), and almsgiving (donating money or possessions to a charitable cause). We deepen our Baptism and conversion. We remind ourselves that through his suffering, death, and resurrection, Jesus redeemed us and reconciled us with God.

For further information: Choose a family or local Church community tradition that takes place during Advent or Lent. Find out how the tradition began and the meaning behind it. How can you apply the practice in your life during this special liturgical season?

Catholics Believe

We must do what we can to repair the harm we have done through our sins to others and to ourselves. See Catechism, #1459.

Think of a penance you have been given in the past. How could that penance have helped you as well as those whom you may have hurt?

_____

_____

_____

When we sin against one member of the community, we sin against the whole community, so we must be reconciled with the Church as well as with God.

We must also try to repair the relationships we have damaged. Maybe we have hurt someone through gossip or untrue statements. Perhaps we vandalized another person's property. Through our Act of Contrition, we must express the desire to make things right. During the Sacrament of Reconciliation, the priest will suggest a **penance,** prayers or acts we can perform to try to repair the harm caused by our sins.

The priest offers us **absolution,** or forgiveness for our sins, in the name of the "Father, the Son, and the Holy Spirit." He speaks the words of absolution on behalf of Jesus.

Rite Response

The Laying on of Hands
The laying on of hands may be part of the Sacrament of Reconciliation. This ritual also plays an important part within other sacraments as well as many other Church rites and blessings. In this way, the Church imitates Jesus, who often touched those he healed.

Effects of
Reconciliation

The effects of the Sacrament of Reconciliation are both spiritual and physical. The spiritual effects include reconciliation with God and others and the Church. This reconciliation can be effective when contact with the person we have hurt does not seem possible. Other effects include peace of mind and conscience, release from guilt and eternal separation from God, and increased spiritual strength.

Many people experience physical effects from reconciliation. Think about what emotional stress can do to the body—increased heart rate, difficulty breathing, lack of energy, headaches, stomach problems, back pain, and so on. When we are healing in spirit, we are healing in body as well. Some people say that after celebrating the Sacrament of Reconciliation, they feel as if a weight has been lifted from their shoulders.

Reconciliation not only provides us with relief from the stress of being at odds with others, it can also give us the opportunity to renew and strengthen our relationships. When friends have worked through a tough situation together, their friendship is stronger, deeper, and more loving because of their reconciling.

Share with your Faith Partner a time when you felt the positive effects of reconciliation.
FaiTH ParTNeRSHiP

Our Global Community

South Africa's Truth and Reconciliation Commission

From 1960 to 1994 the government of South Africa enforced *apartheid*, which made black citizens a lower class within its society. Black South Africans were forced to live in certain areas, called "townships"; they could hold only certain jobs, and they were victims of violence on the part of the government. When apartheid ended, the new government set up the Truth and Reconciliation Commission, which was chaired by Archbishop Desmond Tutu. The commission investigated human rights crimes. It told the truth, in the hope that the truth would lead to reconciliation and forgiveness. Those who stepped forward and admitted to human rights abuses were given *amnesty*—they were pardoned for their crimes. Even though South Africa still has a long way to go, its first step was a big one—realizing that revenge leads to more violence, but reconciliation leads to peace.

Nothing to
Fear

Despite all of the benefits of reconciliation, some people are hesitant to celebrate this sacrament. They may be afraid to talk to the priest, or they may be uncomfortable confessing their sins. Perhaps they are embarrassed. Yes, it can be uncomfortable or even painful to admit the wrong things we have done. But the sins you confess to a priest are between you and God, forever. The priest will never talk about or act on what you have told him; this is referred to as the sacramental seal. Only when we admit what we have done wrong can healing begin.

Reconciliation and Peace

Just as sin results in separation, brokenness, and pain, reconciliation results in togetherness, peace, and healing. When we turn our backs on God, we feel the pain of that separation. Perhaps because we see our family and friends every day, we may feel that pain even more when sin separates us from them. Reconciling with God requires a great deal from us, but God's forgiveness is immediate and complete. Reconciliation with people can be a little more complicated. Once a relationship has been damaged or trust has been broken, reconciliation and forgiveness can take a long time. We must be patient while waiting for forgiveness from the person we have hurt. The sacrament helps us by giving us the forgiveness of God and the Church while we await forgiveness from that person. Instead of giving up on the relationship, we must work at restoring it. When someone asks for forgiveness from us, we must be willing to forgive readily and from our hearts.

Reconciliation is a sign of God's unending love for us. Through it he welcomes us back joyfully. Our challenge is to show that same love in our relationships with God and with others.

Reconciliation takes time and effort, but it pays off in the end with deeper, more loving relationships with God and others and a more peaceful, happy life.

Discuss how young people can live virtuous and reconciling lives. Share your thoughts with your Faith Partner.

FaiTH PaRTNeRSHiP

WRAP UP

- **Being in relationship with others requires a willingness to forgive and to reconcile.**
- **God is always ready to forgive.**
- **We are called to accept the grace to reconcile with God and with those we have hurt.**
- **Through the Sacrament of Reconciliation, our sins are forgiven by God and we are reconciled with the Church community.**

What questions do you have about the content of this chapter?

_____

_____

_____

Around the Group

Discuss the following questions as a group.

What is the most difficult part of reconciling with others? What are the good results of reconciling?

After everyone has had a chance to share his or her responses, come up with a group answer to the first question upon which everyone can agree.

_____

_____

_____

What personal observations do you have about the group discussion and answer?

_____

_____

_____

Briefly...

Some people say that after receiving the Sacrament of Reconciliation they feel as if a weight has been lifted from their shoulders. How is this similar to how you feel when you reconcile with someone? How does this relate to the forgiveness factors that you reflected on at the beginning of this chapter?

_____

_____

_____

SKILLS FOR Christian Living

Examining Conscience

Expressions of Faith–

An important step toward reconciliation is an examination of conscience. Examining your conscience will not only make you aware of the areas of your life in which you have *not* done right, but will also help you see the areas in your life where you *have* done right. You will learn a lot about yourself, and you will come to be more at peace with God. And interestingly, you may begin to examine your words and actions *before* you speak or act.

Scripture

Always be ready to make your defense to anyone who demands from you an accounting for the hope that is in you; yet do it with gentleness and reverence. Keep your conscience clear, so that, when you are maligned, those who abuse you for your good conduct in Christ may be put to shame.

1 Peter 3:15–16 | 6th Sunday of Easter, Cycle A

Skill Steps–

Remember the device for examining conscience? When we examine our conscience, we need to admit what we commit and what we omit.
Here are some key points to remember:

ADMIT
COMMIT
OMIT

- We sin by our words, actions, and thoughts.
- We sin when we intentionally do something we know is wrong.
- We sin when we fail to do something we know would be right.
- An examination of conscience helps us recognize when we have sinned.
- An examination of conscience is the beginning of the reconciliation process.

Skill Builder–

Each of us needs to choose our own style of examining conscience. One person might find inspiration in Scripture, while another person would use relaxing music. Wherever and however you are most comfortable examining your conscience, the most important thing is that you take the time to do it.

What are some things that would help you with an examination of conscience? What things might prevent you from making an honest examination of conscience? List things that would help you and things that would distract you. Use the following words to get started:

music, Bible, candle, being outside or inside

Share your responses and thoughts with your Faith Partner.

FaiTH PaRTNeRSHiP

Would Help	Would Distract

Putting It into Practice-

Select one word from each of the brackets in order to form a helpful examination of conscience:

For example: [When, who, how] have I [hurt, failed to help] someone with my [words, actions, thoughts]?

[When, who, how] have I [hurt, failed to help] someone with my [words, actions, thoughts]?

Answer your question. Then write two or three more examination questions from the bracketed text.

_____

_____

_____

_____

Remember that an examination of conscience is only the first step. It helps us recognize when we have made poor choices. But to be truly sorry for the hurt we have caused, God calls us to identify and change our behavior.

Sometimes we get into the habit of going through the motions without really believing in what we are doing. If you begin to recognize the same sinful choices reappearing frequently, you are only doing half of what God asks of you. Remember that as you put Examining Conscience into practice.

How do you feel about using this skill? Place a check mark next to the phrase that best describes where you are now.

- I'm very comfortable with this type of reflection.

- I'm going to need to work on this.

- I'm not comfortable with personal reflection, and this may be awkward.

Closing Prayer-

Father, your Son taught us how to live a life of virtue. Give us the strength to follow his example. Help us admit when we have sinned, and guide us to reconciliation with you and with others whom we have hurt by our words, actions, thoughts, or failures to act. Amen.

CHAPTER 7

Our Sexuality

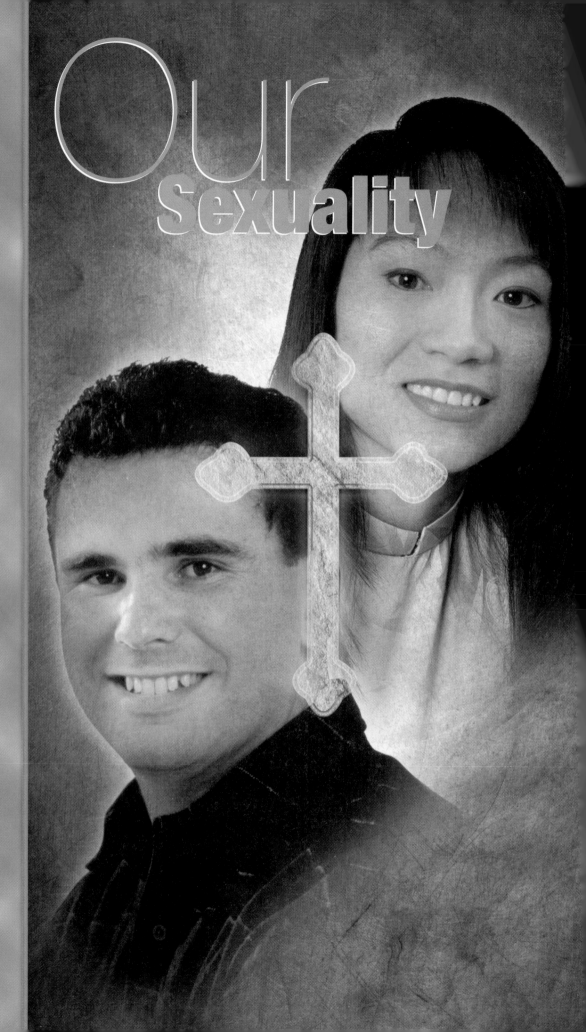

Dear Lord, by your awesome power and goodness you created us male and female. May we cherish this and all our gifts from you, remembering that all we do should glorify you. Amen.

Answer each of the following questions with one of these responses: A. Not at all   B. Very little   C. Somewhat   D. Greatly

How does being a boy or being a girl impact your relationships with . . .

Your teachers or coaches? _____

God? _____

Family members? _____

Your friends? _____

Your class? _____

Members of the other gender? _____

What comes to mind when you see the word *sexuality*?

_____

_____

Gifts from God

Our entire self is a gift from God. But just who are we? We are an incredible combination of physical ability, intellect, spirituality, and emotion. These qualities help define our personalities. As social beings we use our individuality to relate to and work with others.

Another aspect of our individuality springs from our being male or female. And like our intellect, spirituality, emotions, and physical ability, our being male or female is an integral and indistinguishable piece of who we are. We cannot remove any of these qualities, and we cannot totally single out these qualities as to how they individually affect our behavior or experience of life. When we accept ourselves, we can see how all of these qualities are gifts from God.

Sexuality

When we look in the mirror, one thing is unmistakable: we are either male or female. Our gender is the outward sign of our **sexuality,** which includes the ways we think, view life, and express ourselves. It is a very important part of who we are, and it affects virtually every part of who we are.

The physical aspects of our sexuality are the most obvious. The other aspects of our sexuality are less obvious but just as real. For example, recent research has shown that men's and women's brains are somewhat different. The result is that, in general, our thinking patterns differ. Our emotions, as well as our physical development, are affected by the levels of hormones we have from the time of puberty on. Socially, our sexuality affects how we relate to others and how they relate to us. Spiritually, men and women relate to God in somewhat different ways.

There is no set way that one gender acts. Women can be firefighters, and men do not have to hide their feelings. Stereotypes do not allow us to see each other as individuals and they limit opportunities for one gender. We need to recognize stereotypes when we encounter them and confront or look past them.

Catholics Believe

When it is expressed as God intends, sexuality is a source of joy and pleasure, both in body and in spirit. See Catechism, #2362.

How does being male or female bring you joy?

_____

_____

_____

Life to the Fullest

Sexuality is a powerful gift, touching all aspects of our lives. Our **sexual orientation** refers to our attraction to members of the same or the other gender or both genders. The Church, in agreement with most scientific research, teaches that sexual orientation is usually not a free choice. Therefore, a homosexual orientation is not a sin in itself although it is objectively disordered. Homosexual acts are sinful because they do not take place in the true context of marriage and they separate sexual intercourse from **procreation,** bringing new life into the world.

Chastity is a virtue that helps us express our sexuality appropriately according to our vocation. Chastity directs us to make good choices regarding the use of our sexual power. Living a chaste life means having self-control and respecting others. It means knowing that certain sexual activities are appropriate only in the context of marriage. Abstaining from sexual intercourse until marriage is a sign of respect for all those we date and a wonderful expression of love for our future spouses. Chastity ensures that we will not use others as objects. The key to healthy and happy relationships in the future is respectful, loving, chaste relationships now.

Modesty works with chastity to help us respect and honor our privacy and that of others. When we are modest, we avoid extremes in emotions, actions, dress, and language. Popular fashion does not take your privacy or personal dignity into consideration. It is your decision whether to wear a particular type of clothing or to wear your hair a certain way. It is also your decision whether to use inappropriate language, even though doing so may make you seem disrespectful of others rather than cool. Like chastity, modesty takes some effort on our part. Chastity and modesty both require self-discipline and self-control.

Discuss with your Faith Partner why modesty and chastity are important virtues. What makes it a challenge for young people to practice these virtues?

FaiTH PaRTNeRSHiP

A Gospel for Today
In March 1995 Pope John Paul II issued an encyclical called *The Gospel of Life.* This document pointed out the many traditional problems, like poverty and war, as well as contemporary problems, like cloning and other technological breakthroughs, that devalue the dignity of human life.

One issue within the document is that of anti-birth actions and policies. In industrial societies, such as the United States, the birth rate has dropped. Contraception and abortions have contributed largely to this decrease. In developing countries, the population has continued to grow. Because of the poverty in these countries, many of these governments have instituted anti-birth policies that forcibly limit the number of children a family may have. *The Gospel of Life* states that both of these situations are wrong and challenges Catholics to work toward a society that accepts all new life.

For further information: Read about the Church's mission to developing countries. What does the Church recommend to counteract anti-birth policies?

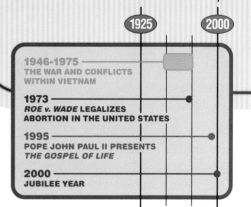

1925   2000

1946-1975
THE WAR AND CONFLICTS WITHIN VIETNAM

1973
ROE v. WADE LEGALIZES ABORTION IN THE UNITED STATES

1995
POPE JOHN PAUL II PRESENTS *THE GOSPEL OF LIFE*

2000
JUBILEE YEAR

WHAT'S THE MESSAGE? Next time you're watching prime-time TV, do some thinking about how sex is presented in the show you're watching. Write your impressions on the lines below.

TV show you watched _____

Do the values expressed by the show match God's values?
_____

What message is this show sending about sex?
_____

Sins Against Chastity

Just as chastity results in healthy relationships, misuse of our sexuality can lead to pain and heartache. Sins that are contrary to chastity include masturbation, pornography, and fornication.

Masturbation is deliberate sexual self-stimulation. It may seem that this act is harmless because it involves one person in private. In actuality it distorts the true meaning of sexuality because it is not life-giving and it does not contribute to the intimacy of marriage.

Pornography is sexually explicit material in magazines, videos, CDs, and other media, including the Internet. It degrades the gift of sexuality, sending the message that people are simply sexual objects and that it is okay to treat them as such.

Fornication is sexual intercourse between two unmarried people. It removes this special physical intimacy from the context of marriage. The physical, emotional, and spiritual consequences of sexual intercourse outside of marriage far outweigh the brief pleasure. Generally, without the loving commitment of marriage, the couple tends to grow apart instead of closer.

Sexual abuse is any sexual contact in which one person uses his or her authority over the other to gain the contact. Situations in which this might occur could be in a teacher-student relationship or employer and employee. Rape is forcing someone to have sexual intercourse without his or her consent. Both of these situations are serious matters. Neither abuse nor rape are ever the fault of the victim.

Sins Against
Marriage

Marriage is a sacred union between a man and a woman, blessed by God. It is a covenant framed by vows of lifetime commitment and fidelity and the acceptance of children. But there are sins that are directly contrary to marriage. Those include **contraception,** and other artificial methods of birth control, *adultery, polygamy,* and *free union.* Contraception is the use of substances or devices to prevent conception, the beginning of a new life. By removing the element of procreation from sexual intercourse, these methods can result in couples using one another as objects instead of respecting each other as partners. Some methods of birth control do not prevent conception; instead they prevent a fertilized egg from implanting in the uterus. This means they are *abortifacient.*

Adultery is a married person having a sexual relationship with someone other than his or her spouse. This violation of the marriage covenant causes separation and pain to all involved. Polygamy is the practice of having multiple husbands or wives at the same time. And free union, or cohabitation, is two people living together in a sexual relationship outside of marriage. As with all sin, these acts have the power to separate people from each other and even from their true selves.

The physical expression of our sexuality is an awesome gift with a great responsibility. The key for us is to respect the precious gift of sex and to pray for the grace to live the kind of life that brings real joy and true happiness.

Opening the Word

2nd Sunday of Ordinary Time, Cycle B

[D]o you not know that your body is a temple of the Holy Spirit within you, which you have from God, and that you are not your own? For you were bought with a price; therefore glorify God in your body. 1 Corinthians 6:19–20

Read *1 Corinthians 6:12–20* as well as *Genesis 1:26–28* and *Genesis 2:18–24.* Choose a passage and paraphrase it to make it most meaningful for you.

_____

_____

_____

Sexuality and Relationships

Our sexuality is so much a part of who we are that it can be difficult to step back and think about how much it affects us and our relationships. Sometimes it can be hard to deal with all the emotions and feelings that result from our sexuality.

You probably relate differently with boys than you do with girls. Maybe you find it easier to talk personally with friends that are your same gender. Or it could be that you share more interests with those friends than with friends of the other gender. The emotions involved in your relationships with members of your own gender are likely different from those with people of the other gender. This difference is natural and healthy. The key for us to remember is that no matter to whom we are relating, we must act with love and respect. We must show modesty in how we dress, act, and talk, and respect the privacy of others. We must remember that our emotions and actions, however strong, need to be controlled. Our actions and behaviors are a matter of choice. Feelings are feelings, neither good nor evil. But what we choose to do with them can be morally right or wrong. We must realize that the consequences of our actions in all aspects of our sexuality can have lifelong impact on ourselves and others.

Reflect on how God's gift of sexuality influences one's relationship with others. Share your thoughts with your Faith Partner.

WRAP UP

- Sexuality is the way we live as men and women.
- The gift of sexuality requires that we respect and care for our bodies and the bodies of others, avoiding harmful situations and practices.
- Chastity and modesty help us use God's gift of sexuality appropriately according to our vocation.
- Respect for self and others should guide us in all our relationships.

What questions do you have about the content of this chapter?

_____

_____

_____

Around the Group

Discuss the following questions as a group.

What are some reasons for misunderstandings between men and women?

What things can we keep in mind to help prevent some of these misunderstandings?

After everyone has had a chance to share his or her responses to the second question, come up with a group answer upon which everyone can agree.

_____

_____

What personal observations do you have about the group discussion and answer?

_____

_____

Briefly...

At the beginning of this chapter, you reflected on the meaning of the word *sexuality.* **Would you answer the question differently now? Why or why not?**

_____

_____

_____

Expressing Affection

Expressions of Faith-

It is natural to have feelings for friends, family, and members of the other gender. But one key to happiness in those relationships is expressing our affection appropriately and thus practicing the virtues of respect and charity.

Scripture

Let love be genuine; hate what is evil, hold fast to what is good.
Romans 12:9

Think About It-

Rank the following situations based on the appropriateness of the affection shown. Use a scale from 1 to 5, with 1 being very appropriate and 5 being very inappropriate.

_____ A boy really likes being around a girl in his class. So he sneaks up behind her and knocks her books out of her hands.

_____ Two boys are best friends. They are constantly punching and pushing on each other. When they are sent to the office for fighting, they say, "We were just goofing around."

_____ A couple goes to a school dance and they kiss during every slow dance.

_____ A girl is sick and out of school for two weeks. A boy in her class sends her a get-well card.

_____ Two girls seem to care about nothing but some boys in their classes. They call the boys on the phone every night.

_____ A girl wants to know a boy in her class better. She asks him if they could sit together at lunch.

Skill Steps-

In expressing affection, the key is to act in a way that is appropriate for the situation and the relationship. We must show respect for the other person and set up boundaries for the relationship.

Make a list of things to keep in mind when expressing affection.

_____

_____

_____

_____

_____

Check It Out-

Place a check mark next to the areas with which you are comfortable.

○ Expressing affection with respectful words

○ Expressing affection to adults in your family

○ Expressing affection to your brother(s) or sister(s)

○ Expressing affection to friends of the same gender

○ Expressing affection to friends of the other gender

○ Expressing affection appropriate to the relationship

> Choose the area in which you may need to change your actions. List some ways you could better express affection in that situation.

_____

_____

_____

_____

Closing Prayer-

God of love, you gave us the gift of sexuality, which helps us grow in love. Assist us in living a life of chastity, modesty, and virtue that respects the dignity of our bodies and those of others. Help us remember that our love for others should mirror your love for us. Amen.

Respecting Life

Jesus, you have the words of everlasting life. You showed us the sacredness of life and relationships. Help us respect the lives of all people, especially those who are unable to defend themselves, from the preborn to the aged. Amen.

Circle the term or terms that mean *sacred* to you.

holy   from God

every day   personal

awesome   mysterious

unexplainable   miraculous

other: _____

What does it mean to say that life is sacred?

_____

_____

_____

_____

Sacred
Creation

"I have called you by name, you are mine."
Isaiah 43:1

God is an awesome God. Our creator existed before time began and will continue to exist after time is no more. Out of nothing he fashioned a vast universe. Picture the sky on a clear night. You can see thousands of stars. There are billions more you cannot see in countless galaxies thousands of light-years apart. Our galaxy, the Milky Way, is one of the smaller ones; our star, the sun, is one of the smallest in the galaxy; and our planet is only one of nine surrounding the sun. Can you imagine the hugeness of it all? Thousands of galaxies, billions of stars, trillions of planets.

All life is from God, and human life, especially, is sacred. Today technological breakthroughs present us with many complex issues, such as cloning and organ transplantation. Through study and prayer we can see beyond the "technology" of these issues and determine whether they respect life or whether they devalue the sacredness of God's creation.

Birth of John the Baptist

Listen to me, O coastlands,
*   pay attention, you peoples from far away!*
The LORD called me before I was born,
*   while I was in my mother's womb he named me.*   Isaiah 49:1

Read *Isaiah 49:1–6* as well as *Exodus 20:13* and *Matthew 10:28–31.* Which passage speaks best to you about the sacredness of life? Why?

_____

_____

_____

Respecting **Life**

Because human life is sacred, we are called to respect and defend the lives of all people. But this is not just an individual responsibility; the community as a whole is called to respect and defend all its members.

If you have ever seen a nature show in which a herd of water buffalo is attacked by lions, you've seen how the herd defends itself. Those who are healthy and strong are driven by instinct to defend the helpless. Humans have free will, as well as instinct. Our responsibility to defend those unable to defend themselves is all the greater.

We are called to practice a **consistent ethic of life,** to realize that human life at all stages is sacred. And so on issues that concern human life, such as abortion, violence, and suicide, the Church calls us to stand on the side of life. This call goes back to the ancient Hebrews. As he gave them the Law, in *Deuteronomy 30:19–20,* God urged the people to choose life.

In every society there are many violations of the sacredness of life, from violent assaults to experiments using fetal tissue. From conception to the end of life, there are any number of ways the gift of life can be devalued. The Fifth Commandment states "You shall not kill." But time and again this commandment is violated. Murder takes many forms. Except to defend one's self or others, any intentional killing of another person is murder, a grave matter.

"IN [GOD'S] HAND IS THE LIFE OF EVERY LIVING THING AND THE BREATH OF EVERY HUMAN BEING."

JOB 12:10

Threats to Life

The first threat against human life is direct **abortion,** the deliberate killing of a preborn baby. Spontaneous abortion, or miscarriage, is the result of natural causes and not the result of an intentional act. Therefore there is no moral decision. A direct abortion, however, is a terrible wrong because it is the willful killing of a human life. It is also wrong to take part in an abortion, such as counseling someone to have one or even just neglecting to act to prevent one. These acts or omissions must be confessed and penance done.

Although some women willingly choose to have an abortion, other women are persuaded or pressured to choose abortion by the baby's father, family members, or friends. These women are told that there is no other way to "solve" their "problem." The Church realizes that reaching out to these women is important if we are to love as Jesus did, recognizing that women who have had abortions (freely or not) are still children of God. Sometimes after an abortion women experience extreme guilt, grief, shame, and anxiety, called *post-abortion trauma*. The Church, through groups like Project Rachel, provides counseling for women who have had abortions.

OUR CHRISTIAN JOURNEY

Living the Message of Life Joseph Cardinal Bernardin, the Archbishop of Chicago from 1982 to 1996, used the image of the "seamless garment" to express his understanding of the consistent ethic of life—that all human life is sacred. As Catholics we are called to stand on the side of life. We must defend life for all people and at all stages. This philosophy became even more real to Cardinal Bernardin when he was diagnosed with cancer in 1994. The cancer would eventually take his life, but not before he became a passionate fighter for the rights of those who were dying. Through homilies, speeches, and his own actions, Bernardin spoke out against euthanasia and physician-assisted suicide, calling us to realize that even suffering has a purpose. His book *The Gift of Peace* made his beliefs clear. This work, a journal kept during his illness, was finished just days before his death.

For further information: Find books and articles written by or dealing with people who have painful or terminal illnesses. How can their outlooks help you with your own times of suffering?

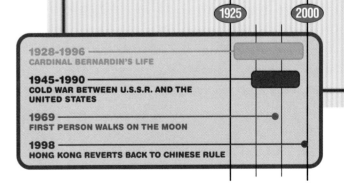

	1925	2000
1928-1996 CARDINAL BERNARDIN'S LIFE		
1945-1990 COLD WAR BETWEEN U.S.S.R. AND THE UNITED STATES		
1969 FIRST PERSON WALKS ON THE MOON		
1998 HONG KONG REVERTS BACK TO CHINESE RULE		

There will be many opportunities in your life to love and learn from new life. Being an uncle or an aunt is just one way we can experience the dignity of a young child.

Another threat against life is **suicide,** the taking of one's own life. When people experience intense emotional pain, suicide may seem to be a solution. In fact, it is only an escape that leaves loved ones with suffering, guilt, and grief. Those who are considering suicide need to be helped to see the value in their lives. We can help our peers by letting them know that they are loved and needed. If we know someone is thinking of suicide, we must get help for the person without delay.

A third assault on the sacredness of life is **euthanasia,** the killing of a person who is ill, disabled, or elderly. Although euthanasia is not yet legal in most of the United States, there are people who promote it. Physician-assisted suicide happens when a doctor provides the means to help a person die. Although the people who commit these acts may have convinced themselves otherwise, euthanasia and physician-assisted suicide are wrong. Dignity exists in all stages of life; even illness, old age, dying, and suffering can have a value. It is not necessary, however, to use extraordinary measures to prolong the process of dying.

Capital punishment is another act usually contrary to the sacredness of life. In many states in the United States, the death penalty is used as punishment for serious crimes such as murder. Some would say that a person who commits murder

deserves death. But the Church teaches differently. When we follow the example of Jesus, we see that he saved all people through his suffering, death, and resurrection. Murderers, too, are saved. They must be punished, but they do not have to be killed. It is not our place to interfere with the person's opportunity to do penance and to strive for forgiveness from those he or she hurt and from God.

War also shows disrespect for life because of the evils and injustices that come with it. An individual does have a right to defend himself or herself, and so does a nation. However, acts of aggression and the use of weapons for the large-scale destruction of civilians are immoral.

With your Faith Partner, list some of the reasons people give in favor of euthanasia or capital punishment. Then work together to explain why these reasons do not follow Church teaching.

Catholics Believe

Human life is sacred. God alone is the Lord of life from beginning to end. No one has the right to end an innocent life.
See Catechism, #2258.

What are ways that some governments violate this teaching?

_____

_____

_____

Violence

Violence in any way devalues life, even if it does not involve the death of a person. Unfortunately, violent acts have become "solutions" for some people who have problems and a way of life for other people who need or want to feel that they belong.

There are times in every person's life when a situation or problem seems to have no solution. Perhaps someone is teased constantly at school and feels he or she has no friends. The situation could grow to the extent that the person sees no end to the loneliness and the teasing. The person might seek revenge by using violence or he or she might try to find friendship in a gang or some other dysfunctional relationship. We need to realize that violent acts and relationships based on violence are never a solution to our problems. There are nonviolent ways to resolve problems; we need to be open to finding them even when that is difficult. Prayer, talking with family members or other trusted adults, or even reading can often help us through difficult times.

Society sometimes sets material items and success above relationships and the sacredness of life. This way of life eventually leads to separation from others. When we set loving relationships as a priority in our lives, we can avoid using violence and instead rely on conflict resolution and other forms of reconciliation to help us with problems in our relationships.

Rite Response

Anointing of the Sick

The Church, through the sacraments, celebrates important stages in our lives. Anointing of the Sick is a celebration of God's healing power. This sacrament can be celebrated for elderly people, any time a person is seriously ill or hurt, and certainly when a person is near death. Through the prayers and blessings of this rite, the Church affirms its belief that every stage of life is sacred. Those who are very sick or are dying have dignity and are loved by God. This sacrament allows us to show them how much we love them and how much we desire peace and healing for them. And though they may not be healed physically, this rite gives them spiritual healing and grace.

The Seamless Garment

Joseph Cardinal Bernardin's teaching on the "seamless garment" applies not just to life or death issues but to all our relationships. Our view of the dignity and sacredness of life affects how we treat others. If we view life as less than sacred, we may be more tempted to treat others with disrespect. We disrespect others any time we see them only as what they mean to us, such as burdens to be tolerated or as objects to be enjoyed, not as God's highest creation.

If we value each life as sacred, we will more likely treat others with love and dignity. When we can look into the eyes of others—no matter who they are or what they have done—and see God, we cannot see those lives as less than sacred. When we see others with God's eyes, anger is replaced by forgiveness. When all people view life as sacred, violence in any form won't happen. When we work with others and not against them, we are signs of the kingdom of God.

Discuss with your Faith Partner how the consistent ethic of life affects our responsibilities toward ourselves, other individuals, and the community.

FaiTH PaRTNeRSHiP

WRAP UP

- •Human life is sacred.
- •The Church calls us to respect and defend the health and well-being of all children of God.
- •The Church upholds the consistent ethic of life.

What questions do you have about the content of this chapter?

_____

_____

_____

Around the Group

Discuss the following question as a group.

What could your group do to show your school, parish, or community how you value and respect human life?

After everyone has had a chance to share his or her responses, come up with a group answer upon which everyone can agree.

_____
_____
_____
_____
_____

What personal observations do you have about the group discussion and answer?

_____
_____
_____
_____
_____
_____

Briefly...

At the beginning of this chapter, you reflected on the term *sacred.* **How do you think your relationships with your family and friends would be affected if you saw them as sacred?**

_____
_____
_____

Expressing Affection

Expressions of Faith-

There are many ways we can express affection. Some ways are physical, like hugging or holding hands, or even giving a pat on the back. The aspect of touch is a key part of relationships. During our entire life, we need to be touched. Touch can establish firm bonds in many of our relationships, allowing us to give and receive love and support.

Scripture

Love does no wrong to a neighbor; therefore, love is the fulfilling of the law.
Romans 13:10 23rd Sunday of Ordinary Time, Cycle A

Skill Steps-

Remember that when we express affection, we must be respectful of others and our relationships and be aware of boundaries.
Here are some key points to remember:

● Everyone needs both to give and receive affection.

● There are appropriate and inappropriate ways to express affection.

● Expressing affection must always start with the belief that every human is sacred and deserves the respect due a child of God.

● Expressing affection well includes respect, sensitivity, setting boundaries, and chastity.

Skill Builder-

Review the situations below from Chapter 7. Where people have expressed affection inappropriately, think of ways these people can better deal with the situation.

Knocking books out of someone's hands

_____

Punching and pushing someone

_____

Kissing through all the slow dances

_____

Sending a get-well card to a classmate

_____

Calling boys or girls on the phone every night

_____

Now, based on what you have read in this chapter, think of some other things to keep in mind about expressing affection.

_____

_____

_____

_____

_____

Putting It into Practice-

This is for your eyes only!

Identify someone to whom you would like to express affection in your life right now—maybe a family member, a peer, or a close friend.

Who? (use a symbol or initials to maintain privacy)

_____

How will you do it?

_____
_____
_____

What are some things to keep in mind in this case?

_____
_____
_____
_____

If we remain sensitive to others as individuals, it won't be as difficult to express affection appropriately.

Give yourself a grade on your actions. Would you pass a class about expressing affection? How much thought do you need to apply toward this skill?

_____
_____
_____
_____
_____
_____
_____
_____
_____
_____
_____

Whether you are close to the goal of appropriate expression of affection or whether you have work to do, love is worth the effort!

Closing Prayer-

God our Father, you have created us for love. Sometimes we fail to live that love. Help us respect all people because you have given them life. Guide our leaders in dealing with issues such as abortion, capital punishment, euthanasia, and war. Guide each of us as well, that we might respect life in all its stages. In Jesus' name. Amen.

We Are One Body

Jesus, you said that whatever we do to the least of your brothers and sisters, we do to you. Help us realize that the injustice of this world is sinful. Give us the courage and the strength to do something about it. In your name we pray. Amen.

84

Answer the following questions on the lines provided.

What are some types of people you consider "losers"?

_____

_____

What are some types of people you consider "winners"?

_____

_____

How is Jesus' view of people different from your view?

_____

_____

All Have Dignity

The final event of the Summer Olympics is the marathon. For 26.2 miles runners compete against each other, the weather, the road, and their previous times. The winner's name will be listed in the record books, but the rest of the runners are usually forgotten. However, the most memorable performance of the 1996 Olympic Men's Marathon came not from the winner, but from the runner in last place.

Baser Wasiqi from Afghanistan completed the race more than three hours after the winner had crossed the finish line. The streets of Atlanta had emptied, and the Olympic Stadium had been cleared to prepare for the closing ceremonies. As Wasiqi entered the stadium to run his final laps, a band there practicing for the closing event moved over to the track and began playing the Afghani national anthem. Others in the stadium stopped what they were doing and lined the track, cheering. Wasiqi gained a great deal of respect that day because of his persistence and perseverance. Sometimes the people the world brands as "losers" are, in fact, the real champions. Their struggles give us hope. Baser Wasiqi may have lost this race, but he "won" respect. We all have the right to be treated with dignity and respect, just as they were given to Wasiqi.

One Body in Christ

Each of us is called to live according to God's law of love. Loving others includes caring for others. Because of this law we are called to pursue goals that are good for all people. This means trying to improve unsatisfactory conditions and to create situations that allow people, either as groups or individuals, to reach their full potential. When we pursue these situations, we give people the chance to use and develop their gifts and talents. Paul's First Letter to the Corinthians speaks of the importance of recognizing every person's gifts. (See *1 Corinthians 12:1–31*.) The analogy is made between the community and the body. Just as all the parts of the body work together for the good of the whole body, so, too, the members of the Church are the Body of Christ, and the good of the entire Body depends on acknowledging the value of each member.

In a society that promotes the good of the individual, humanity's basic needs must be met and basic human rights protected. Our basic needs are the things we need to survive on earth. Pope John XXIII listed food, clothing, shelter, health care, rest, and social services as our basic needs. In addition, we have a right to the means to attain these basic needs, including equal opportunity, education, and employment. Our basic rights are given by God and protected by society.

With your Faith Partner, illustrate on a poster board the Body of Christ. Use people you know and their good works to fill in the parts of the body.

Opening the Word

34th Sunday of Ordinary Time, Cycle A

"Truly I tell you, just as you did it to one of the least of these who are members of my family, you did it to me." **Matthew 25:40**

Read *Matthew 25:31–46* as well as *Proverbs 14:31* and *Luke 14:12–14*. Choose a verse from one of these passages and design a motto from it.

Water DENIED

The human person should be the first priority of every organization and government, no matter how big or small. But what does this mean? On one level, it means a group of students respecting each others' differences. For families it means seeing each member as an individual and fostering potential and responsibility. The profits of companies must be shared with the workers in wages and benefits. Governments should make and enforce laws that protect individuals and groups, as well as provide for the good of all.

Focus On

Works of Mercy

The Spiritual Works of Mercy
Warn the sinner
Teach the ignorant
Counsel the doubtful
Comfort the sorrowful
Bear wrongs patiently
Forgive injuries
Pray for the living and the dead

The Corporal Works of Mercy
Feed the hungry
Give drink to the thirsty
Clothe the naked
Shelter the homeless
Visit the sick
Visit the imprisoned
Bury the dead

Justice DENIED

Natural **Moral Law**

Just as we are called as individuals to live God's law of love, we must be sure our society reflects that ideal. The goal of society should be to promote virtue and to strive for justice. Society must be guided by the **natural moral law,** the moral sense that allows us to use our reason to figure out right from wrong. This law applies to people of all backgrounds and cultures. If we follow this law that comes from deep within us, we will work toward the basic needs of all and protect their basic rights. We will be in **solidarity** with others. A community in solidarity recognizes its oneness with God and has a sense of belonging to and being responsible for one another.

However, we sometimes work against solidarity. Friends sometimes put negative peer pressure on each other to engage in self-destructive or anti-social activities. Some groups, such as supremacy groups, are drawn together by shared hatred. Some government leaders resort to terrorism and mass murder or allow slavery or starvation of their own citizens. When individuals fail each other, separation and pain result; but when governments fail to live according to the natural moral law, the results are even more devastating. In the last century alone, tens of millions of people have died at the hands of their own governments or invading armies.

DENIED **Compassion**

Jesus had compassion for those in misery. In fact, he most closely identified with the least important people. So the Church, too, must take up the cause of those who are poor.

See Catechism, #2448.

What does it mean to take up the cause of those who are poor?

_____

_____

_____

_____

The Church and
Social Justice

Proclaiming the gospel, the Church has a long history of standing on the side of **social justice.** Social justice teachings cover basic human rights, equality, economic fairness, and the treatment of those who are poor. Other issues include the environment, war, and helping developing nations.

The Christian response, including that of the Catholic Church, begins with the law of love and the Beatitudes. The Church is obligated to work for justice and do works of charity. The charitable act is to feed a hungry person. The just act is to ask and then respond to why someone is hungry in our society of abundance. The demands of justice must be satisfied first of all. That which is already due in justice is not to be offered as a gift of charity.

When we attend to the needs of others, we give them what is theirs, not ours. We are paying a debt of justice. The Church is obligated to act in situations of injustice. And so it engages in **works of mercy** modeled after the example of Jesus. Through both the Corporal

and Spiritual Works of Mercy, the Church seeks to erase the suffering caused when the natural moral law is not followed by others.

The Corporal Works of Mercy are concerned with meeting the physical needs of others. The Church has missionaries around the world feeding, clothing, sheltering, and healing those in need. Religious orders like the Sisters of Charity reach out to those most in need. The Church has founded countless

hospitals, health clinics, soup kitchens, and food pantries. Organizations like the Society of Saint Vincent de Paul exist to provide food, shelter, and hope for people who are homeless.

The Spiritual Works of Mercy include those things that minister to the spiritual, or inner, needs of people. These needs, such as gaining knowledge and being comforted, are just as vital as our physical needs of being sheltered and having health care. To serve these inner needs, the Church provides services such as counseling centers and crisis pregnancy centers. Anywhere there is a need, we can find the Church at work, seeking to help meet the needs of people.

Every one of us is called to do our part to ensure that all people are treated with dignity and respect. Injustice is a universal problem. Justice starts with each one of us.

OUR CHRISTIAN JOURNEY

Defending the Oppressed

Archbishop Oscar Romero was born in El Salvador in 1917. He was ordained a priest in 1942 and appointed Archbishop of San Salvador, the capital of El Salvador, in 1977. When one of his priests was murdered, Romero was surprised that there was no official investigation. He soon realized that high-ranking members of the government were corrupt and probably responsible for the murder. At that time, death squads roamed El Salvador, killing those who spoke out against the government. Several priests, nuns, and missionaries were killed, along with countless Salvadoran citizens. Archbishop Romero spoke out, preaching that Jesus stands on the side of those who are oppressed. As talk of violent revolution grew among the people, Archbishop Romero received death threats. But he continued to preach, reminding the people that death does not come without resurrection. On March 24, 1980, Romero was assassinated while celebrating Mass. Today his teachings still challenge us to promote social justice.

For further information: Read about other religious who spoke against government oppression. How were they similar to Archbishop Romero?

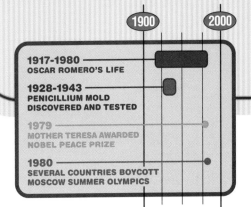

1900   2000

1917-1980
OSCAR ROMERO'S LIFE

1928-1943
PENICILLIUM MOLD
DISCOVERED AND TESTED

1979
MOTHER TERESA AWARDED
NOBEL PEACE PRIZE

1980
SEVERAL COUNTRIES BOYCOTT
MOSCOW SUMMER OLYMPICS

You Can Do It, Too

World peace, hunger, and homelessness are complex issues. It's easy and perhaps comfortable to think that we cannot do anything to solve them. After all, no one person can change the whole planet. If we adopt that attitude, we are defeated before we have even begun and we do nothing.

If we do nothing, we reject Jesus' command to serve and to love. So we must figure out what one person can do to make a difference. The first step is to realize that we *can* make a difference. You make a difference to the people in your life right now. What you say or don't say and what you do or don't do affects the people around you. You might not make a difference in India, but you make a difference in your school, your neighborhood, and your family.

The next step is to find out what service opportunities exist in your community. Your teacher, youth minister, and pastor are all good people to ask. Perhaps your parish has an outreach ministry or a food pantry. There are plenty of things even a teenager can do. But you won't know until you look around and ask some questions.

Discuss with your Faith Partner what two works of mercy you can practice.

FaiTH PaRTNeRSHiP

WRAP UP

• Social, political, and economic injustices exist in the world.

• Every person has a vocation to love.

• Christ has called us to works of justice and charity.

• For Christians justice is an obligation, not a choice.

• The Spiritual and Corporal Works of Mercy help us respond to others' needs.

What questions do you have about the content of this chapter?

_____

_____

_____

Around the Group

Discuss the following question as a group.

What are some specific ways your group can work for justice?

After everyone has had a chance to share his or her responses, come up with a group answer upon which everyone can agree.

_____
_____
_____
_____

What personal observations do you have about the group discussion and answer?

_____
_____
_____
_____

Briefly...

At the beginning of this chapter, you reflected on how you defined winners and losers compared to the way Jesus thought. How can you strive to treat people as Jesus did?

_____
_____

Offering Solidarity

Expressions of Faith-

In our vocation to love, we are called to stand in solidarity with those who are poor or oppressed. Some oppression may be due to the action of your peers. Solidarity requires strengthening the connections between people rather than further dividing them. Justice, compassion, and hope are concrete virtues for developing solidarity.

Scripture

"[F]or I was hungry and you gave me food, I was thirsty and you gave me something to drink, I was a stranger and you welcomed me, I was naked and you gave me clothing, I was sick and you took care of me, I was in prison and you visited me."

Matthew 25:35–36

34th Sunday of Ordinary Time, Cycle A

Think About It-

Think about the Spiritual Works of Mercy—teaching, praying, counseling, and comforting. You already practice these works, such as when you listen to a friend or sit with someone who needs a shoulder to cry on.

Circle all the phrases below that describe what you do when others are in need.

Try to understand

Ask them what's wrong

Don't care   Listen

Let them know I'm there for them

Try to be kind   Make fun of them

Offer comfort

Be sympathetic   Talk about my own problems

Change the subject   Other: _____

Skill Steps-

We are expected to offer solidarity, to be willing to help those in need. But being willing and knowing how are two different things.

The skill of Offering Solidarity consists of four actions involving your eyes, ears, hands, and hearts.

We must have EYES TO SEE. We must *look around and notice* who needs help or is being treated unfairly.

We must have EARS TO HEAR. We must take the time to *listen to the story* of those who need help or fair treatment. Listening is the first step to understanding a problem.

We must have HANDS TO HELP. We must *actually do something* to support those in need.

We must have HEARTS TO HOLD. We must *pray* or *fast* for a group in need. We often pray for things that matter only to ourselves. Fasting is sacrificing something we often take for granted, such as food, spending money, or watching TV, as a reminder that others are in need all the time. Jesus told his apostles that some things can be brought about only through prayer. (See *Mark 9:29.*)

Check It Out-

Place a check mark next to the statements that apply to you.

◯ I try to notice when others are in need.

◯ I spend more time listening than talking to someone who needs me.

◯ I do what it takes to help out those in need.

◯ I pray or fast for those who suffer.

Which of the above actions do I already do? Which of these actions do I need to work on?

_____

_____

_____

_____

_____

Closing Prayer-

God our Father, you are Father to us all. Help us see the needs of others, listen to the stories of the suffering, and take action on their behalf. Send your Spirit upon us to give us the strength and courage it takes to be people of service, people of love. In Jesus' name. Amen.

God our Father, you lead us and guide us. You call us to live the gospel and to witness to your love. Send your Spirit that we might be the hands, ears, and voice of Christ here on earth. Amen.

Our Prophetic Role

Answer the following questions.

What do you value or treasure the most?

_____

_____

_____

How does what you value affect your life?

_____

_____

_____

How do you use your talents to make your community a better place to be?

_____

_____

_____

Good News

Think about something great that has happened to you. Maybe you got a really good test grade. Perhaps you and your team played an exceptional game. Or maybe you did very well at a music competition. Whatever great thing happened to you, it would have been very difficult to keep quiet about it. More than likely, you told everyone you could. Good news is meant to be shared.

The Gospel according to Mark tells of just such a thing. After Jesus heals a man with leprosy, he tells the leper to keep the healing a secret. The leper tells everyone he sees what Jesus has done for him. (See *Mark 1:40–45.*)

Jesus has saved us from something worse. He saved us from the power of sin and everlasting death. His death and resurrection have made it possible for us to have eternal life with God. In Baptism we take part in the Paschal mystery. We are blessed with a peace and joy that we simply must share, like any good news. In fact, one sign of a strong relationship with God is that we can't help but share it in word and action.

Witness for God

Like the leper in the Gospel story, we must share our experience of Jesus. The grace and faith we have received from God cannot be hidden. The peace that comes from confessing sin and being reconciled can change our lives. The freedom we experience when we respect God's gifts of life, sexuality, and community moves us to help others experience that same freedom.

In short, we must **witness** to God at work in our lives. To witness is to share our beliefs and values through our words or actions. Many people are very good at talking about their faith, telling others about their relationship with Jesus. These people and many others who may not say a lot about their faith do a wonderful job of living their faith. Everyone can be a faith-filled model for others to follow. The Church, the Body of Christ, needs the gifts of all its members.

No matter where we are in our faith journeys, we are called by God. We are called to holiness. When we respond to this call, we are aware of the **common good;** we consider the needs of others as well as ourselves before we act. That means treating others fairly and with the respect they deserve. It means honoring the authority of our adult family members and teachers. It means not making fun of classmates or talking about them behind their backs.

We are also called to exercise good **stewardship,** taking care of God's gifts of creation. Recycling our glass, aluminum and steel products, and newspapers is an easy way to begin environmental stewardship. But there are other ways we can create less solid waste, such as using both sides of a sheet of paper and giving away books, clothes, or other things we don't want or use. We can also learn what the environmental issues are. Water quality problems or shortages may be calling us to relearn usage habits and think of the big picture. Good stewardship also requires that we use our gifts wisely. When we care for creation, we respect other things and the earth itself as part of God's gift not only to us, but to the generations that will follow us.

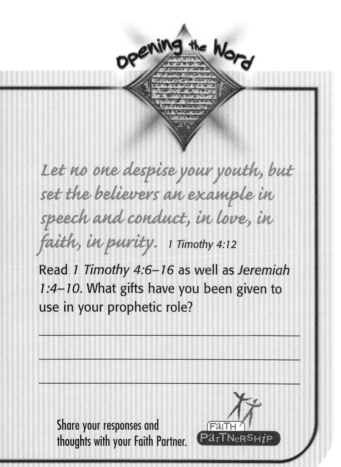

Opening the Word

Let no one despise your youth, but set the believers an example in speech and conduct, in love, in faith, in purity. 1 Timothy 4:12

Read *1 Timothy 4:6–16* as well as *Jeremiah 1:4–10*. What gifts have you been given to use in your prophetic role?

_____

_____

_____

Share your responses and thoughts with your Faith Partner.

FaiTH PaRTNeRSHiP

The Call

Besides being witnesses and stewards, we are also called to be **prophets,** to speak God's message to others. Throughout salvation history God has chosen ordinary, and sometimes young, people to bring his word to the world. These people became extraordinary because they listened to God's call in their lives.

Some prophets, like Samuel and Jeremiah, were barely teenagers when they were first called by God. David was a youth when he slew Goliath, a mighty Philistine warrior. Moses had a speech impediment. Many of the saints and martyrs honored by our Church were young people when they died, and none of them were perfect.

Being a saint or a prophet is not something to work for in the future. It is about listening to God now and always. We do not have to be perfect to be holy or to share our faith; we do have to be open to God's love and help, or grace. It has been said that saints are merely sinners who repent and keep trying to do what is right and good. The same can be said for us.

Media Message

CONSUMPTION OF GOODS Television shows, radio programs, and magazines are funded by selling advertisements. We are constantly exposed to commercials and print ads that tell us we need to get rid of those jeans or shoes from last year and buy new ones. Sometimes we believe this, while other times we can see through the tempting ad. There are ads directed at everyone in all walks of life. According to advertisers, we need new cars, new dishes, and new toys, even if our cars, dishes, and toys are still usable. This lifestyle of material gain and consumption is in opposition to good stewardship.

What is the prophetic response to these messages?

_____

_____

_____

In the space below, design your own ad that tells how to rejuvenate or newly appreciate items that you already own.

The faithful must see the relationship between their rights and duties as members of the Church and as members of humanity. Their Christian conscience should guide every activity. See Catechism, #912.

List two ways our society would be different if everyone followed this teaching.

_____

_____

_____

Not an **Easy Road**

Being a prophet is not easy. God might ask you to do things you do not want to do. You will want to resist, to ignore the call. Jonah, in the Old Testament, literally tried to run away from the place to which God was calling him. But Jonah could find no peace until he did what God asked him to do. (See *Jonah 1:1–3.*)

You may doubt yourself and think nobody will listen to you. Maybe you think that if you start challenging the wrongs that people are doing and telling them to change, they will think you are uncool and will start making fun of you. Jeremiah feared that people would not listen to him because he was young. God made it clear to him that he would put the words in Jeremiah's mouth. God assured Jeremiah that he would be with him. God's promises to Jeremiah are also true for us. (See *Jeremiah 1:4–8.*) Sometimes you will fail to reach people. When that happens, you must ask for God's help and perhaps try new approaches.

If you see someone cheating on a test, you have a few options. You can do nothing. You can tell the cheater that you saw him or her cheating and that you will tell the teacher if he or she does not admit to it. You can tell the teacher. There are probably other options you can think of. The first option helps no one.

The second is a little more like the prophet, letting a person know that he or she is wrong and needs to do something about it. However, if this would result in violence toward you or if the other person is not going to own up to the wrong, the third option may also be a prophetic response. Some wrongdoings, such as drug use or weapon possession, must always be brought to the attention of those who can correct it.

Some prophets challenge society as a whole. Jesus challenged individual people to change their lives, but he also challenged some of the scribes and Pharisees, who were overly concerned with the details of the law. In doing so, Jesus was seen as a troublemaker by some of the leaders, who then conspired to have him crucified.

In modern times, Martin Luther King Jr. challenged white people in the United States to change their discriminatory attitudes and policies. When he spoke the truth about racism, he angered many people. He was assassinated in 1968, but not before his words had taken hold in the hearts of many people and changes had begun to take place.

Today, think about the way people who speak out against the falsehood of "safe sex" or against abortion or the death penalty are sometimes ridiculed or labeled "extremists." Speaking the truth can be tough. However, when we respond to our call as followers of Christ by standing up for what we believe, speaking the truth, and living a life of character and virtue, we will eventually be respected. People may disagree with us, but if we speak the truth in love, we will one day be seen as people of conviction and courage.

A Faithful Servant

Born in Domrémy, France, Joan of Arc claimed to hear voices from an early age. She identified these voices as Saint Michael, Saint Catherine of Alexandria, and Saint Margaret of Antioch. In 1428 these voices told Joan to go to the king of France and help him reconquer his kingdom. The English king and the French Duke of Burgundy had conspired to claim France for England.

After overcoming much opposition, seventeen-year-old Joan was given a small army, with which she won the Battle of Orléans. It was the first of a series of amazing military successes, during which the French king was re-crowned.

In 1430 Joan was captured by soldiers loyal to the French Duke of Burgundy and sold to the English. After an unfair trial she was convicted of heresy. Some historians believe that Joan was abandoned by those she helped. She was burned at the stake on May 30, 1431. Thirty years after her death, Joan was cleared of all charges, and in 1920 she was canonized a saint.

For further information: Look into other events during the 1400s. This was a time not only of great discovery and invention, but also of grave disease and war.

1400	1475

1400–1468
JOHANNES GUTENBERG'S LIFE

1403
CHINA BEGINS SEA ROUTES TO INDIA AND AFRICA

1412–1431
JOAN OF ARC'S LIFE

1414–1417
COUNCIL OF CONSTANCE

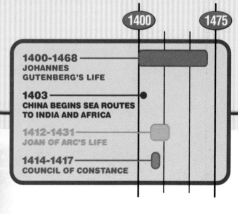

Our **Job**

Being a prophet is a tough job, but we are all called to be prophets. When we doubt that we are able to do the job, we must remember that God does not ask us to do the impossible. God has given us the tools we need to speak his truth. He has given us time, talents, and treasure.

Time is precious. We must live each moment, each day, to the fullest and to the best. We must find balance between being so busy that we are stressed out and having time to waste. Sleep and play are necessary and important, but so are the things we can do to benefit others. We can fill our free time with unproductive activities or with meaningful acts of personal growth, like reading to learn new things, or acts of service to others, like helping a sibling with homework.

Talents are given to us for the glory of God and the good of others. Whether our talents lie in the arts, athletics, or relating to others, they can be used to promote good or ill. Accepting the role of prophet requires that we use these talents to challenge the wrongs in our communities.

Our treasure includes those things that are of value to us. Our treasure can be family members or friends. It can also be money and material possessions. When we make God a part of our relationships, those relationships will be truly life-giving. We must use our money and possessions wisely, trying not to do what is destructive or wasteful. With the proper attitude, these things won't get in the way of our relationships with God and other people.

When we give God our time, talents, and treasure, he will return it to us generously in blessings and gifts.

Discuss with your Faith Partner your own participation in the common good of society.

FaiTH
PaRTNeRSHiP

WRAP UP

- As followers of Christ we are called to be prophets.
- We must challenge society to work toward bringing God's kingdom to its fullness by cooperating with God's grace.
- We must work to promote attitudes and laws that support the common good.

What questions do you have about the content of this chapter?

_____

_____

_____

Around the Group

Discuss the following question as a group.

What do you think society would be like if more people responded to the call to be prophets?

After everyone has had a chance to share his or her responses, come up with a group answer upon which everyone can agree.

_____
_____
_____

What personal observations do you have about the group discussion and answer?

_____
_____
_____
_____

Briefly...

At the beginning of this chapter, you reflected on using your talents. Based on what you have learned, how can you use your talents to make your community a better place to be?

_____
_____
_____
_____

Offering Solidarity

![SKILLS FOR Christian Living]

Expressions of Faith-

The Church is called to be prophetic, to bring to the world God's message of justice, compassion, and hope. It is also called to confront those people and social structures that fail to promote the common good. We can offer solidarity as individuals, but we are called to do it in community as well.

Scripture

Beloved, let us love one another, because love is from God; everyone who loves is born of God and knows God. Whoever does not love does not know God, for God is love.

1 John 4:7–8   Sixth Sunday of Easter, Cycle B

Skill Steps-

Remember the four actions that are a part of Offering Solidarity. We must have EYES TO SEE those in need and EARS TO HEAR the stories of those who suffer. We must have HANDS TO HELP, doing something to help those who need us. We must have HEARTS TO HOLD, praying and fasting for those whom we wish to help.

Here are some key points to remember:

- We are all related.
- Jesus taught us that we should be as concerned about the common good as we are about our personal good.
- God will judge us by how much we care for others.
- The communities to which we belong must offer solidarity and make an impact on injustice.

Skill Builder-

With a partner, focus on the steps of Offering Solidarity. First, take time for each of you to think of a person or group whom you think is being treated unfairly. Then take turns sharing your ideas. Ask each other questions if necessary. After sharing, brainstorm together ways that you could help the persons or groups— remembering works of mercy may get you started. And last, talk with your partner about persons or groups for whom you can pray or fast.

Putting It into Practice-

Complete the following statements.

As a member of my school community, I can encourage solidarity by _____.

As a member of my family, I can help my family offer solidarity by _____.

As a member of _____, I can encourage this community to offer solidarity to _____ by _____.

The skill of Offering Solidarity can be difficult to master, but there are many benefits. In a way, the skill is summed up in the Prayer of Saint Francis in the call to offer consolation, understanding, and love before seeking those things ourselves. Offering solidarity goes against our selfish whims and the tendency of communities to sometimes "look out for number one" while ignoring the needs of others. As hard as it may be to walk in another's shoes, the Christian life calls us to do just that.

In addition to school and family, of what communities are you a part?

_____
_____
_____
_____

How could you use your EYES, EARS, HANDS, and HEART to make these communities even better than they are now?

_____
_____
_____
_____

Closing Prayer-

Lord God, you call each one of us to be prophets, to speak your words to those in our lives, and to confront evil when we see it. Grant us the courage to speak with conviction, to live in solidarity with others, and to bless you always with all we do. We ask this through Jesus our brother and Savior. Amen.

Prayers and **Resources**

The Lord's Prayer

Our Father, who art in heaven,
hallowed be thy name;
thy kingdom come;
thy will be done on earth as it is in heaven.
Give us this day our daily bread;
and forgive us our trespasses
as we forgive those who trespass against us;
and lead us not into temptation,
but deliver us from evil.
Amen.

Hail Mary

Hail, Mary, full of grace,
the Lord is with you!
Blessed are you among women,
and blessed is the fruit of your womb, Jesus.
Holy Mary, Mother of God,
pray for us sinners,
now and at the hour of our death.
Amen.

THE TEN COMMANDMENTS

1. I am the Lord your God. You shall not have strange gods before me.

2. You shall not take the name of the Lord your God in vain.

3. Remember to keep holy the Lord's day.

4. Honor your father and your mother.

5. You shall not kill.

6. You shall not commit adultery.

7. You shall not steal.

8. You shall not bear false witness against your neighbor.

9. You shall not covet your neighbor's wife.

10. You shall not covet your neighbor's goods.

THE BEATITUDES

Blessed are the poor in spirit,
for theirs is the kingdom
of heaven.

Blessed are they who mourn,
for they will be comforted.

Blessed are the meek,
for they will inherit the land.

Blessed are they who hunger and
thirst for righteousness,
for they will be satisfied.

Blessed are the merciful,
for they will be shown mercy.

Blessed are the clean of heart,
for they will see God.

Blessed are the peacemakers,
for they will be called children
of God.

Blessed are they who are persecuted
for the sake of righteousness,
for theirs is the kingdom
of heaven.

(Matthew 5:3–10)

Glory to the Father (Doxology)

Glory to the Father, and to the Son,
and to the Holy Spirit:
as it was in the beginning, is now,
and will be for ever.
Amen.

Gifts of the Holy Spirit

Wisdom
Understanding
Right judgment (Counsel)
Courage (Fortitude)
Knowledge
Reverence (Piety)
Wonder and awe (Fear of the Lord)

Fruits of the Spirit

Charity
Joy
Peace
Patience
Kindness
Goodness
Generosity
Gentleness
Faithfulness
Modesty
Self-control
Chastity

Act of Contrition

My God,
I am sorry for my sins with all my heart.
In choosing to do wrong
and failing to do good,
I have sinned against you
whom I should love above all things.
I firmly intend, with your help,
to do penance,
to sin no more,
and to avoid whatever leads me to sin.
Our Savior Jesus Christ
suffered and died for us.
In his name, my God, have mercy.

Works of Mercy

Corporal (for the body)
Feed the hungry.
Give drink to the thirsty.
Clothe the naked.
Shelter the homeless.
Visit the sick.
Visit the imprisoned.
Bury the dead.

Spiritual (for the spirit)
Warn the sinner.
Teach the ignorant.
Counsel the doubtful.
Comfort the sorrowful.
Bear wrongs patiently.
Forgive injuries.
Pray for the living and the dead.

PRECEPTS OF THE CHURCH

1. Take part in the Mass on Sundays and holy days. Keep these days holy and avoid unnecessary work.

2. Celebrate the Sacrament of Reconciliation at least once a year if there is serious sin.

3. Receive Holy Communion at least once a year during Easter time.

4. Fast and abstain on days of penance.

5. Give your time, gifts, and money to support the Church.

The Apostles' Creed

I believe in God, the Father almighty,
  creator of heaven and earth.
I believe in Jesus Christ, his only Son,
  our Lord.
    He was conceived by the power of the
    Holy Spirit
      and born of the Virgin Mary.
    He suffered under Pontius Pilate,
      was crucified, died, and was buried.
    He descended to the dead.
    On the third day, he rose again.
He ascended into heaven,
    and is seated at the right hand
    of the Father.
  He will come again to judge the
    living and the dead.
I believe in the Holy Spirit,
  the holy catholic Church,
  the communion of saints,
  the forgiveness of sins,
  the resurrection of the body,
  and life everlasting. Amen.

The Nicene Creed

We believe in one God,
  the Father, the Almighty,
  maker of heaven and earth,
  of all that is, seen and unseen.
We believe in one Lord, Jesus Christ,
  the only Son of God,
  eternally begotten of the Father,
  God from God, Light from Light,
  true God from true God,
  begotten, not made, one in Being
    with the Father.
  Through him all things were made.
  For us men and for our salvation
    he came down from heaven:
  by the power of the Holy Spirit
    he was born of the Virgin Mary,
    and became man.
  For our sake he was crucified under
    Pontius Pilate;
  he suffered, died, and was buried.
  On the third day he rose again
    in fulfillment of the Scriptures;
he ascended into heaven
    and is seated at the right hand
      of the Father.
  He will come again in glory to judge
    the living and the dead,
    and his kingdom will have no end.
We believe in the Holy Spirit, the Lord,
  the giver of life,
  who proceeds from the Father and
    the Son.
  With the Father and the Son he is
    worshiped and glorified.
  He has spoken through the Prophets.
We believe in one holy catholic and
  apostolic Church.
We acknowledge one baptism for the
  forgiveness of sins.
We look for the resurrection
  of the dead,
  and the life of the world to come.
Amen.

The Liturgical Year

In the liturgical year the Church celebrates Jesus' life, death, resurrection, and ascension through its seasons and holy days. The liturgical year begins with the First Sunday of Advent.

The readings for the entire Church year are contained in the Lectionary. Readings for Sundays and solemnities of the Lord are placed in a three-year rotation—Cycle A, Cycle B, and Cycle C.

The Season of Advent begins in late November or early December. During Advent we recall the first coming of the Son of God into human history, and we prepare for the coming of Christ—in our hearts, in history, and at the end of time. The liturgical color for Advent is violet.

On Christmas we celebrate the Incarnation, the Son of God becoming one of us. The color for Christmas is white, a symbol of celebration and life in Christ. (Any time white is used, gold may be used.)

Lent is the season of prayer and sacrifice that begins with Ash Wednesday and lasts about forty days. Lent has always been a time of repentance through prayer, fasting, and almsgiving. The liturgical color for Lent is purple, a symbol of penance.

Easter is the high point of the liturgical year because it celebrates Jesus' resurrection from the dead. The week beginning with Palm Sunday is called Holy Week. Lent ends on Holy Thursday evening, when the Easter Triduum begins. The Triduum, or "three holy days," includes the observance of Holy Thursday, Good Friday, and the Easter Vigil on Holy Saturday. The liturgical color for the Easter Season is white, a symbol of our joy in experiencing new life in Christ. The Easter Season lasts about seven weeks (fifty days).

At Pentecost, we celebrate the gift of the Holy Spirit sent to the followers of Jesus gathered in the upper room in Jerusalem. The liturgical color for Pentecost is red, a symbol of the tongues as of fire on Pentecost and of how Christ and some of his followers (such as the early Christian martyrs) sacrificed their lives for love of God.

The majority of the liturgical year is called Ordinary Time, a time when the Church community reflects on what it means to walk in the footsteps of Jesus. The liturgical color for Ordinary Time is green, a symbol of hope and growth.

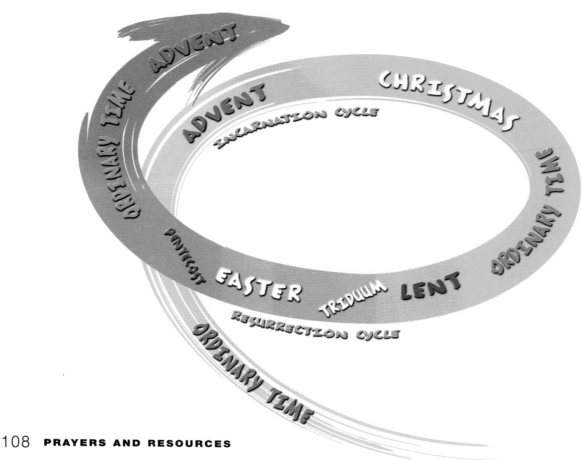

Glossary

A **abortion** — The death of an unborn baby; *spontaneous abortion*, or *miscarriage*, occurs when the unborn baby dies of natural causes; *direct abortion*, any intentional action taken purposely to cause the death of the unborn baby, is a serious sin.

absolution — The forgiveness of sin we receive from God through the Church in the Sacrament of Reconciliation.

authority — Those with the power and responsibility to lead others.

B **Beatitudes** — Sayings of Jesus (*Matthew 5:3–10*) that sum up the way to live in God's kingdom and that point the way to true happiness. The word *beatitude* means "blessedness."

C **capital punishment** — The death penalty; taking the life of a person as punishment for a serious crime such as murder.

chastity — The virtue that helps a person express sexuality appropriately according to his or her vocation.

common good — That which will benefit the entire community. As Christians we are called to perform works for the common good. Working for the common good means that we consider the needs and rights of others before we act.

concupiscence — An inclination toward evil.

conscience — The gift from God that helps us know the difference between right and wrong and choose what is right. Conscience, free will, grace, and reason work together to help us in our decision making.

consequences — The physical, spiritual, emotional, and social results of one's choices.

consistent ethic of life — The belief that all life is sacred because all life was created by God, and the practice that follows from this belief.

contraception — Practices, substances, or devices used to prevent the joining of a sperm cell and an egg cell.

contrition — The deep sorrow and the resolve to do better that we feel when we have sinned; contrition moves us to turn our lives toward God.

conversion — The process of turning away from sin and evil and turning toward God.

D **dignity** — The quality of being worthy of respect that comes from our having been created in God's image.

domestic Church — The Church as it exists within the family.

E **equality** — The state of all humans created in God's image, each deserving respect.

euthanasia — Deliberately causing the death of a person who is ill, disabled, or elderly, or assisting such a person in committing suicide.

F **faith** — The gift given to us by God that moves us to seek him out and believe in him.

fornication — Consensual sexual intercourse between two unmarried people.

free will — The God-given ability to choose between good and evil.

G **grace** — God's life in us through the Holy Spirit, freely given; our loving relationship with God; the free and undeserved help God gives us so that we may respond to the call to holiness.

M **magisterium** — The teaching authority of the Catholic Church, given by Christ through the Holy Spirit and found in the bishops in union with the pope and the priests, who are their coworkers.

modesty — The virtue that respects, honors, and protects privacy; the quality of avoiding extremes of emotion, action, dress, and language.

morality — The way we put our beliefs into action for good.

mortal sin — A freely chosen grave act, attitude, or omission of action that breaks off our relationship with God.

N natural moral law — The moral sense that allows humans to distinguish right from wrong by the use of reason; the natural moral law is universal and transcends cultural differences.

O original sin — The first humans' choice to disobey God and the condition that became a part of human nature whereby we are deprived of original holiness and justice; only Jesus and Mary, his mother, were free of original sin.

P penance — Prayers and actions undertaken to help us, in Christ make up for the harm our sins have caused.

precepts of the Church — Some of the important duties of Catholics. The word precept means "teaching" or "guidance."

procreation — Participating with God in bringing new life into the world; openness to conceiving children.

prophet — A person called by God to speak God's message to humans.

R reconciliation — Bringing together people who have been separated; making peace; celebrating forgiveness, as in the Sacrament of Reconciliation.

S sexual orientation — A person's feelings or attraction toward persons of the same or the other gender or both genders.

sexuality — The way in which we live (physically, mentally, emotionally, socially, spiritually) as gendered persons, male or female.

sin — Turning away from God and failing to love; a deliberate wrong choice to do something contrary to God's law.

social justice — Giving each person his or her due regardless of education, race, gender, or background because each person is a child of God.

social sin — Failing as a community or society or to create just conditions to give others what is due to them.

solidarity — The principle of oneness in the family of God; belonging to and being responsible for one another.

stewardship — Responsible care for creation.

suicide — Taking one's own life.

T temptation — The urge or attraction to do what we know is wrong.

Ten Commandments — The summing up of the moral prescriptions of God's Law given as part of the covenant at Sinai. The first three commandments explain our responsibilities to God, and the last seven commandments explain our responsibilities to our neighbor.

V venial sin — An act, attitude, or omission that weakens but does not break off our relationship with God.

vice — A habit or practice of wrong acts that leads us to sin and away from God and others.

virtue — A habit or practice of goodness that helps us grow in love for God and others.

W witness — Sharing one's beliefs and values in words and actions.

works of mercy — Actions modeled after the life of Jesus that show justice, love, and peace. The Corporal Works of Mercy are actions of care for the physical needs of others, while the Spiritual Works of Mercy are actions of care for the spiritual needs of others.

Index